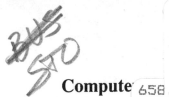

Compute

Macmillan Information Systems Series

Series Editor: Professor I. O. Angell

Computer Security Within Organizations

Adrian R. Warman

Department of Business Information Systems
Bournemouth University

MACMILLAN

First published 1993 by
THE MACMILLAN PRESS LTD
Houndmills, Basingstoke, Hampshire RG21 2XS
and London
Companies and representatives
throughout the world

ISBN 0–333–57727–2

A catalogue record for this book is available
from the British Library.

Printed in Hong Kong

Contents

Preface

Important: this book is designed to provide a summary of some aspects of the subject matter covered. It does not purport to be comprehensive or to render legal advice.

This book is aimed at managers and those studying management, the people for whom computer systems are simply another tool amongst many others that can be applied to the tasks of running an organization.

The objective of this book is to examine the concepts of computer security from managerial and organizational perspectives. As a consequence, there is very little discussion about technical issues such as data encryption mechanisms or operating system domain partitioning, because these are operational issues that need not be addressed by management. The book is not intended to supply a checklist of security topics, as these are provided in other excellent texts.

However, an understanding of how operational issues affect the usage of computers and information systems is very much of interest to managers, and it is this that forms the theme of this book.

The book begins with a consideration of the current situation. An overview of basic security concepts is provided in chapter one, before moving on to look at the way in which problems with technology have come about. Chapter two suggests that the very nature of technology actively contributes to the problems, not least because of the way in which computer systems are developed and utilized. The system development process has a significant effect upon the security of the final system. Chapter three looks first at general development methods, before considering the specifics of secure system development.

The discussion then turns to the social and management aspects of computer security. The increasing strategic value of information and information processing systems means that managers must consider them much more carefully than before. Chapter four considers information technology security from the organizational and management perspective. Security mechanisms can be viewed as serious constraints upon work activities, and even intrusions upon the personal privacy of users. If computer security is to be feasible, at the very least it will require the understanding and active support of all those it affects. There is a need to spread the message to all those involved - and yet to do so may represent a problem in its own right. Chapter five looks into some of these issues.

Legislation has a profound influence on what is permitted on a national and international level, and inevitably affects organizational computer systems. Chapter six considers some of the legal issues. Finally, chapter seven is a speculative discussion of remaining issues such as the effectiveness of controls, and also suggests a number of ways in which the discipline of computer security may change over the next few years.

Acknowledgements

IBM, OS/2 and CUA is a trademark of International Business Machines Corporation.

Lotus and 1-2-3 are registered trademarks of Lotus Development Corporation.

Microsoft is a registered trademark and Windows is a trademark of Microsoft Corporation.

UNIX is a trademark of AT&T Bell Laboratories.

The newspaper headline discussed on page 103 is reproduced courtesy of Evening Standard Company Ltd.

This book would not have been possible without the help and support of the many people who provided material, advice and encouragement. I want to thank them all. In particular, I would like to thank my wife Sue for her patience and understanding while this book grew from a short list of chapters to the final manuscript. As well as excusing me from some of the more tiresome daily chores, she also read through every chapter, offering invaluable advice and constructive criticism. Accordingly, I dedicate this book to Sue, with my love.

1 Basic concepts

- Security: the eternal problem
- How active threats are implemented
- The CIA model
- Summary

Before considering who is affected by computer security, and its organizational consequences, we need to look at the basic concepts of security and threats to systems.

Throughout the discussion, mention will be made of both computer systems and information systems. It is important and useful to make an informal distinction between the two. Computer systems are a collection of technology components, such as hardware and software or programs. Most computer systems of any value will also be information systems; if they are not, it will be hard to justify any expenditure, past or future, on the computer equipment.

Information systems are any collection of components that can be used for collecting, processing, storing and providing information. Information systems do not necessarily depend on the presence of a computer system. A filing cabinet is an example of a very simple information system. Information can be stored in it, and a limited degree of processing can occur by creating and using cross-references.

However, the emphasis on computer security in this book means that we will mostly be concerned with information systems that are computer-based.

Security: the eternal problem

The fundamental issue which computer security specialists attempt to address is that computer-based information systems can be misused or suffer from failures. This can result in a number of threats to the organization or to information users, such as non-availability of the information to those who need it, or alternatively the provision of information to those who should not have it. Accordingly, when implementing computer security measures, we are attempting to deal with these threats by working towards certain objectives.

The first of these objectives is *prevention*, which is the task of trying to stop instances of misuse or failures from happening in the first place. Examples would include ensuring that unauthorized users are not be able to gain access to an information system, or protecting valuable data from deletion. For prevention to be possible requires an understanding of how and why the various threats can occur; and then identifying and implementing appropriate measures that will prohibit or at least constrain their occurrence.

It may be that the first goal of prevention cannot be achieved. This could be because the prevention methods turn out to be, or are suspected to be, inadequate. Alternatively, they may be considered too expensive to justify in the light of the perceived threat. In either situation, the secondary aim will be to try to limit the damage or losses that can result from a threat. Thus, we allow for the possibility that an authorized user might accidentally delete valuable data by providing data recovery mechanisms - or backups - that will enable the computer system operators to retrieve as much of the material as possible.

In practice, it is not always possible to return to the exact point at which the data was deleted so that the information can be recovered. However, in most situations it should be possible to provide a restoration to a point as recent as the end of the last working day. The importance of making backups cannot be overstated, a point which was forcibly demonstrated to the author on the day of his research degree examination.

Approximately 30 minutes before the examination was due to begin, a slip of the fingers while typing a command meant that the complete set of demonstration files was deleted from the computer. Fortunately, a complete backup of all the relevant files had been taken by the author only five minutes previously, so it was a comparatively simple matter to recover all the work. However, it was an educational experience of a kind that the author has no wish to repeat.

The paradox for computer security specialists is that absolute security can never be achieved, yet must continually be sought. The reality is that as long as computer systems are utilized, there will continue to be the opportunity for accidental or deliberate system failure. The primary goal of prevention is an ideal that simply cannot be achieved in all instances. In practice, the best that computer system users or owners can hope for is to achieve the secondary goal and make an attempt towards some limited degree of prevention. Unfortunately, the measures and techniques that may be applied to minimise threats will themselves be constrained according to the perceived threats and costs of preventing the identified threats.

Furthermore, while the availability of technology can be of some help in working towards improved security of computer systems, the technology cannot of itself be the entire solution. As we will see, it is essential that both the people who interact with the system, and the environment where interaction occurs, are also considered. This is because people are capable of finding ways around technological security mechanisms, as is amply demonstrated by the various examples given in this book.

The nature of information system threats

The first step is to consider the possible sources of threats to which computer systems may be exposed. We may define a threat as a potential action or event and, if the threat actually occurs, the result will be some form of loss. In everyday terms, a loss may be the sudden and perhaps unexpected absence of access to a resource. An obvious example is in a bank, where there is the threat of stealing cash. If a bank raid takes place, it can result in a loss of money, so that a financial resource may no longer available to the bank manager or customers.

The ways in which losses may occur can only be identified by considering, with judicious use of imagination, the possible situations where threats might arise. For example, writing a password down on a piece of paper could result in a loss if someone else picks up the paper and uses the password. Some losses may occur from the combined effects of multiple threats. In one case, an engineering firm was at risk of going out of business as a result of combined threats. A hardware fault in a new computer system delivered by a well known manufacturer meant that as data was entered into a database, the cross-referencing information was not being recorded correctly. If the engineering firm had been making backups of the information regularly, and as advised by the manufacturer, then the errors in the cross-referencing could have been dealt with comparatively easily by writing a special program to examine the changes made from day to day so as to correctly reconstruct the cross-references. However, no backups of the data had been taken by the computer operators. The combined effect of these two failures meant that the entire database had to be manually repaired by a team of specialist computer engineers over an extended and costly period. Thus the combination of two problems resulted in a major problem for the engineering firm.

Given the almost unlimited number of possible threats to consider, it is helpful to simplify the problems. For example, instances of threats to systems may be divided into two domains: passive or accidental, and active or deliberate. Passive threats may be further subdivided into two sub-domains: natural or physical disasters, and accidental errors. Active threats refer to deliberate or malicious activity.

Threats that arise from the passive domain cannot readily be predicted or avoided, while those from the active domain *can* in theory be predicted and avoided, given sufficient consideration and preparation. For both domains, the degree of protection required in order to provide sufficient defence will be determined by the balance between the cost and the perceived benefit of the protection measures.

A special category of threat exists within the passive domain, and that is any threat which derives from environmental circumstances. An information system designer can do very little about these.

All computer and information system threats arise from one of the above domains. This means that while many threats could be predicted in advance, there is always the possibility of 'new threats' arising from within a specific domain. For example, although obvious with hindsight, few people would have been able to successfully predict the following documented threats to systems: electrocution of hardware by lightning; cable chewing by rats and mice; and physical abuse of equipment by kicking, punching, stabbings and shootings.

Natural or physical disasters

Threats such as fires, floods, power outages and component failures, are examples of threats or hazards which can affect computer systems, simply due to geography or environment. Other examples would include threats arising from earthquakes and other seismic activity, and environmental aspects such as humidity and temperature.

There is very little that can be done to avoid threats of this kind. At best, the computer system implementation would have to incorporate suitable fall-back measures to promote some degree of fault-tolerance. In the event of a threat occurring, the system might then be able to accommodate some or even all of the effects of the threat with less harm.

Smaller computer systems, such as PCs and workstations, are generally less susceptible to some environmental threats for a number of reasons. Being smaller, and hence portable or relatively easily relocated, they have been designed to tolerate a moderate degree of rough-handling. Typically, they do not generate much heat from the electrical components, and so built-in fans and cooling systems are normally adequate for most requirements, rather than requiring additional external refrigeration or ventilation systems. However, microscopic dust and smoke particles can accumulate over time, perhaps encouraged by the static fields often associated with electrical systems. These particles can soon start to 'clog-up' the equipment, and so reduce cooling-system efficiency with resulting greater stresses on the physical system itself.

Certain other threats are independent of geography or environment. Fire is a perennial threat that will always pose a problem where there are combustible materials. Computer systems are often situated near to large quantities of paper-based documentation and printers or plotters; yet the electrical nature of the equipment can mean that certain kinds of fire-inhibition measures may not be appropriate. It is particularly important that rubbish from such sources should not be allowed to accumulate. As well as being a valuable source of information about the organization, the piles of accumulated paper represent a significant fire hazard in their own right.

Liverpool City Council in the UK experienced this sort of problem in April 1991. A fire was caused when a heating unit developed a fault and set fire to the carpet. The main destruction was not the result of flames but smoke, which caused £300,000 worth of damage. Although there were no computers in the room, it did hold backup tapes which were destroyed. Fortunately, the backups were spare copies of tapes held off-site, so no information was lost.

Perhaps surprisingly, flooding may also be a threat, not least due to the common practice of placing computer system hardware in the controlled environment of a basement - often for reasons of fire protection. One organization suffered problems during any wet weather, as the increased pressure in the drainage and sewage system resulted in back flows through the toilets. Owing to the proximity of the computer room, this resulted in very unpleasant floods. Computer systems do not normally react well when exposed to water, so that the simple but effective water sprinklers, often used to damp down fires, cannot be utilized in a computer room.

In April 1992, flooding brought a huge section of Chicago's business district to a standstill for several days. Power was cut off from the district after water from the Chicago River burst through a wall damaged by workers into a 100-year-old tunnel system that runs under the city. Some 250 million gallons of water rushed through the hole, and power to over 200 buildings had to be disconnected to prevent the possibility of fires caused by short-circuits. For the Chicago Board of Trade, the effect was that their computerised transaction board was closed for two and a half days.

A similar problem in the same month left a Buckinghamshire hospital in the UK without a data centre after its mainframe was drowned in a flash flood. Wycombe General Hospital's mainframe was out of service for almost a week when rainwater pipes running through the data centre burst.

The weight of the hardware is often omitted as a consideration, but the floor structure must be sufficient to handle the system weight. This is particularly important if 'raised floors' are to be employed in order to provide under-floor cable ways for linking multiple computers and peripherals together.

This also introduces another threat. The large number of power, control and data cables that are often required and collected in a computer room may all contribute to extremely peculiar effects from electromagnetic interference. During transmission from computer to computer along cables, data is represented using varying voltages. Electromagnetic interference can obscure these voltages, so that the data is not so clearly defined at the receiving end. This makes data transmission errors more common.

Power supply failure is a major source of computer system threat, in that a number of faults can occur: sags - where voltages drop below acceptable levels, surges - where voltages exceed acceptable levels, spikes - where sudden combinations of sags and surges occur, and other difficulties such as frequency variations, interference and complete power cuts. These can cause serious difficulties for computer systems, which require a continual supply of power. In the UK, 88% of electricity consumers experience voltage sags that exceed a 10% drop below the nominal value, and the disturbances can last for a cumulative total of 1.5 hours per year.

A number of measures can be taken to try to protect a computer system's power supply. The most straightforward is some form of Uninterruptible Power Supply (UPS). In simple terms, this is a collection of large rechargeable batteries that can provide an adequate electricity supply for a short but valuable period of time while the computers are shutdown in an ordered manner. As soon as the main electricity supply fails, the UPS begins working, and starts an alarm to warn the system operators that action should be taken as soon as possible. Unfortunately, the larger the computer system, the greater the power requirement. In many cases, the specification of the UPS chosen is not actually sufficient to provide enough time for the computer system to be halted in a 'safe' state.

Accidental errors

Humans can certainly contribute to the variety of accidental threats to information systems. Major difficulties can result from smoking, eating or drinking near to computer hardware and magnetic media. Less obvious but equally problematic is the danger of becoming too familiar with the system - there are many cases of people failing to take full and adequate copies of their work because they mistakenly suppose that the system is always going to be available to them, upon demand.

Similarly, it is astonishingly easy to make changes to data or files that you had not intended to. As has already been suggested, when data is deleted, recovery may not be straightforward even for technically competent users. Indeed, it may even be the case that the more experienced a user is, or the greater the familiarity with the system, the more likely it is that the user can make a mistake through not thinking about the task being performed.

Some of these difficulties are illustrated in the UNIX operating system, and are sometimes cited as one reason why UNIX is not considered to be 'user-friendly'. UNIX was originally developed *by* computer specialists *for* computer specialists, and as a result, many of its commands are notoriously cryptic and terse. This is a result of deliberate choice, in that many users familiar with the UNIX system are quite happy to use two- or three-letter commands in preference to the equivalent but longer and apparently more time-consuming commands that are required for other operating systems on mini- or mainframe computers.

The UNIX operating system also makes an important additional assumption. This is that users entering commands always know exactly what they want to do. Consequently, very few UNIX commands entered by users are ever questioned by the computer at all - even if the command just given will result in the erasure of all the working information in the system, or indeed the deletion of the entire operating system.

When discussing natural or physical threats, the need for a continuous supply of electricity was highlighted. Power supply failures also arise in the accidental error domain, as there are threats from simple sources such as power cables being cut by building contractors, or even plugs pulled out accidentally by office colleagues.

A variation on the theme of accidental errors concerns insecure disposal procedures. Inevitably, organizations will generate material and information that could be considered sensitive in some fashion. For example, a university should take care during the preparation of examination papers to ensure that no student has an unfair advantage from seeing papers beforehand. This means that draft work on questions cannot simply be discarded in the same way as drafts for other work. Similarly, a commercial organization attempting to carry out a take-over may wish to keep its plans secret to minimise competition or difficulties with asset valuations. Another organization may be planning a new venture, or the launch of a new product, and would like to keep its plans secret from any competition.

The dilemma is that when computer systems are introduced into an organization, they often make it very easy to alter documents and other information. Far from providing the once loudly praised 'paper-less office', computers will generate enormous quantities of data on paper, often with only small variations from version to version. Simple observation indicates that a surprisingly large number of users working on a document will happily reprint a large document, even if only a single minor change was made, perhaps on the last page of the document.

The potential for rapidly accumulating piles of outdated versions of documents and information means that there can also be severe difficulties associated with disposal. Firstly, the user must be sure that the documents or items of information being discarded are no longer required; in other words, more accurate or more up-to-date versions have been retained. Secondly, the user must ensure that material that is discarded cannot be acquired or processed by unauthorized individuals, as it may contain sensitive information. This is a particularly important consideration if paper is being recycled, for example where both sides of a sheet are to be used before it is discarded.

There have been cases where information was thought to have been destroyed, but in fact was still accessible to outsiders. One of the most interesting examples occurred during the major scandal of the Reagan administration, the 1988 'Iran-Contra' affair, and concerned Colonel Oliver North. He assumed that simple deletion of material from a White House computer-based information system meant that the data could not be recovered. He was mistaken.

Information can often be obtained from the most obscure sources. Even today, careful study of a typewriter ribbon can reveal exactly what documents were typed using that ribbon. Pressure of a pen or pencil on a notepad while writing will leave impressions on the underlying sheets that can be reconstructed. The information that can be obtained from such sources is so important that it even has a name to identify the process: garbology. The name derives from the activity of searching garbage cans for discarded items such as memos, computer print-outs, manuals, transparencies or slides used in formal presentations, and so on.

Finally, one of the most common causes of accidental errors is from confusing instructions or procedures. This is particularly true following the introduction of a new system, or one with only minor differences from an existing system. The lack of familiarity with a system can cause difficulties for people, especially if it involves new terminology or concepts that they have never had to work with before, whereas a system with only small changes may lull users into a false sense of security as they perform old tasks on the new system.

Deliberate or malicious actions

These are actions which may be planned in advance, or which are known to be wrong, unlawful, or at least detrimental to the organization. They could derive from outsider interaction, such as hackers obtaining unauthorized access or entry; or from industrial spies carrying out analysis of waste materials. Alternatively, insiders may bear ill-will to the organization, for example disgruntled employees or curious observers from other internal departments. We may define an insider as someone who has authorized access to a system, while an outsider does not have authorized access.

These definitions mean that the same person can be both an insider and an outsider, dependent upon the circumstances. For example, students at a college may be described as insiders in the sense that they are allowed access to computers for project work and report writing, but outsiders in the sense that they are not allowed to access the computers or files which hold examination papers or marks. Identifying the extent to which someone is an insider or an outsider is helpful in determining the permissions and authority an individual may be given.

Regardless of whether an insider or outsider is involved, a malicious action is usually intended to result in some form of gain for the person responsible. The gain may be financial, or simply one of satisfaction at having 'beaten the system'. Regardless of what form this gain takes, the perpetrator will often prefer that both the method used and its effects should remain as secret as possible, for as long as possible. Their hope is that the mechanism will be left undisturbed and undetected. This is either to prevent discovery of their actions, or to make later reuse much easier.

Perhaps the classic method for obtaining financial gain is to implement the so-called 'salami attack'. This is a near-apocryphal concept where additional code is entered into a computer by a system developer or operator. The salami code quietly removes almost insignificant quantities from monetary values being processed - and often converted - by the computer system.

In effect, the code performs surreptitiously what commercial arbitrageurs may perform openly, taking advantage of the small numeric errors that naturally accumulate during financial conversions, and reallocating them elsewhere. A slight variation on the theme is for a programmer to add a 10% 'fee' to account charges. For example, if a bank account holder would be charged £10 for a particular service, a £1 fee is added to the bill, and the money moved to another account set up by the programmer.

In practice, salami attacks are rare because they are easy to detect. All financial dealings are invariably closely monitored with multiple audit and cross-referencing mechanisms, that cannot be bypassed very easily. Such checks would quickly reveal the effects of a salami program.

Continuing the theme of simplifying the issues by breaking them down into simpler problems, we can observe that malicious actions manifest themselves in one of two forms: overt or covert actions.

Overt actions may be described as involving 'brute force', concentrating upon seeking a probably destructive route to the desired objects of attention, regardless of any damage caused on the way. These are fairly easy to detect after the event, and this in itself gives some information to the protector of the computer system, albeit as a way of preventing further cases from occurring.

Examples of this would include theft of computer and other office equipment, the absence of which should normally be detected very quickly.

Covert actions are more subtle, and do not corrupt the system so quickly or so obviously. In particular, where a computer-based information system is being used, then a variety of automated techniques may be employed.

Techniques of this kind are particularly effective at enabling the individual to obtain data or information secretly. This is because it is not possible to identify an attribute or property of data that changes as a result of the data being duplicated or revealed to an unauthorized recipient. In other words, the fact that data has been viewed does not in any way change the *nature* of that data, and so the fact that it has been revealed cannot be detected by simple inspection of the original material.

An everyday example would be the photocopying of documentation, in that the original remains almost unaffected no matter how many copies are taken. Similarly, a program or file which is stored electronically on a disk or tape can be duplicated simply by replicating the arrangement of electromagnetic particles on another disk. The replication process need not alter the arrangement of information on the original disk in any way. It is for this reason that backups are so easy to make, and similarly that software piracy, as described in the chapter on legislation, is possible.

It is astonishingly easy to design straightforward covert technology mechanisms that can reveal a great deal of information to those acquainted with the specific methods employed. A very simple example can be found in research surveys that are regularly carried out for organizations by post. Often, it is desired that the respondent to an interview remain anonymous, even to the interviewer. And yet, the nature of the interviewee may be of interest and relevance to the work of the researcher.

Consequently, the interviewing organization may wish to incorporate some form of identification mark within the reply material. Any ID or number on the questionnaire sheet would be spotted quickly, and a prudent respondent wishing to retain anonymity may well reply in a different format anyway.

However, by enclosing a SAE, the interviewing organization would be able to code the return *address* in a unique manner that would be most unlikely to arouse suspicion, and this would be more than adequate to provide the desired information.

One method that might be used builds upon the fact that a surprisingly large quantity of information can be encoded by precise use of 'binary switches' within data. The presence or absence of a very simple item, such as a full stop character, may correspond to a 'yes' or 'no' answer to a question. Table 1 shows an example, where the presence or absence of a full stop after the title

Table 1: The use of 'binary switches' to represent information

Coding	Interpretation	Meaning
Mr J. Smith	No full stop after 'Mr' First name is initial only	Small firm International firm
Mr. J. Smith	Full stop after 'Mr' First name is initial only	Big firm International firm
Mr. John Smith	Full stop after 'Mr' First name is full	Big firm National firm

'Mr' could indicate that the person works for a small firm (no full stop), or for a big firm (there is a full stop). More complex groups of binary switches could be used to provide other information which might be used for a variety of purposes.

When computer systems are brought into consideration, it becomes a very simple matter for even a relatively inexperienced system developer to incorporate code into the system that would allow such covert information to be conveyed to any user by means of otherwise normal reports, but which is only meaningful (or even detectable) to those who are aware of the key to identification.

For example, most computers can produce printouts showing the amount of work that has been done by an individual, or the quantity of data held on a particular fixed disk. This information will often be presented in the form of a table. It would be easy for a programmer to arrange that the layout of the table changes very slightly to reflect changing information, in the manner illustrated in table 1.

It must be admitted that such simple form of this particular technique can easily be bypassed. In the questionnaire example above, the alert interviewee does not have to use the supplied SAE. However, a common mistake is to return the questionnaire using internal mail, which frequently utilizes a postal franking mechanism that most conveniently adds the address or logo of the organization.

How active threats are implemented

Having identified the main categories of threats to computer systems, we can now turn to examine the domain of active threats in more detail. Unlike passive threats, which have no malign intent, active threats are intended to harm the target computer system, or at the very least provide some form of gain for the attacker.

Active threats can be carried out in two ways. Firstly by non-automated or direct action on the part of the attacker, and secondly by automated or indirect action.

Non-automated or direct system penetration

Here, the penetrator assumes the identity of an authorized individual in order to perform an unauthorized function. This is based on replicating one or more of the following characteristics, in order of increasing difficulty:

- Something the user knows.
- Something the user has.
- Something the user is.

The first method requires the penetrator to convince the computer that he is an authorized user, by replicating evidence and supplying it to the computer, where the evidence is something that only an authorized user could know. The most obvious example would be that of the computer hacker. The access is granted by the computer system if the hacker can provide sufficient evidence to the computer that he *is* an authorized user. The easiest evidence that a hacker would try to provide would be something that the genuine user knows, generally a password.

Much more difficult to replicate would be something that the authorized user has, such as a special key that the computer can recognise. The key may be as simple as an ordinary metal key inserted into a lock, up to a much more complicated electronic device that can generate a uniquely coded response when challenged by the computer system.

The final and most complex characteristic is something that the authorized user is, for example he is 1.80 m tall exactly, or weighs precisely 70 kg. A more useful example would be for a computer to recognise the unique patterns of a user's fingerprints, or the blood vessel arrangement on the retina of the user's eye. Precise measures of this kind are extremely difficult for an unauthorized individual to replicate. Unfortunately, these measures are also rather expensive and somewhat complex to provide for all but the most sensitive computer system.

Automated or indirect system penetration

This form of active threat is more complex, and often involves the cooperation of the computer system in facilitating its own demise. In simple terms, a tool within the computer is used to attack or further open a known weak point in the overall system. Attempts may be made continuously and repeatedly, or only upon demand.

The objective of the attempts may be to gain access to the system in order to deny other users any form of service from the computer system. Alternatively, the intruder may wish to corrupt items of data, or to get hold of secret information. An example of this occurred at the end of 1989, when over 20,000 computer users, mostly in the UK, received a floppy disk claiming to hold information on research into the Aids virus. The disks came from a nonexistent organization, the PC Cyborg Corporation. But the disks also contained a program which altered the directory structure in the computer, so rendering all files inaccessible. The computer could only be made to work again on payment of a fee of $378, sent to an address in Panama. The unusual and widespread nature of this particular threat made it a headline feature in some newspapers (see page 103).

The use of an automated tool means that the person responsible for the threat does not have to be in direct contact or control at all times. This helps to conceal the identity of the perpetrator.

The sources of automated threats to an information system come in four major categories: Worms, Trojan Horses, Logic Bombs and Viruses.

Worms Worm programs have been understood and implemented since the early days of computing, particularly with respect to computer networks and distributed systems. A worm program - strictly speaking a tapeworm program - is one which begins its life by taking up residence on a particular machine. Once established, it proceeds to makes copies of itself to send to other machines which are attached in some way to the original host machine.

Thus a worm program is one that will reproduce itself throughout the computer system, normally with one entity per host. Once installed, the worms can cooperate with each other in scavenging for scarce resources, such as available memory or disk storage space, or in more advanced systems to help identify less heavily-loaded hosts which might then assist in performing some data processing tasks.

Unfortunately, malignant forms of these worms exist. Examples documented in case studies have caused machine overloads following a population explosion, or deliberate removal or denial of service from the computer. If the worms fail to limit their reproduction to a single entity per host, or attempt to take over excessive processing resources, then they can rapidly cause a slow-down for the entire computer system, and in extreme cases cause complete failure and shutdown by overloading. It was precisely this sort of situation that was caused by the notorious 'Internet Worm' of 1988.

The worm was created by a student, Robert Morris Jr, and inserted into a huge network of computers called the Internet on the evening of 2 November 1988. It proceeded to replicate itself and began to infect other computers which were connected to the Internet. The worm had its own list of over 400 passwords to help break into other computer systems, plus a sophisticated algorithm to help it to find and learn passwords that it did not already have. From the outset, it was designed to be difficult to detect and hard to eradicate once detected.

Morris used his terminal at Cornell University to launch the worm, but made it look as if the worm had originated from a terminal at the University of Berkeley in California. Several hours later, he noticed that his terminal was very slow to respond to commands. He immediately realised that the worm was replicating itself at a fantastic speed, much faster than anticipated. As a result, it was causing congestion in his computer system and many others. This congestion meant that he was unable to prevent the worm from spreading further, because he could not issue the appropriate commands quickly enough; and also prevented him from issuing warning messages across the already overcrowded network message system. The Computer Virus Industry Association, a group interested in security, subsequently claimed that Morris's worm infected around 6,000 computers. The Association further estimated that the total cost of removing the worm, including the lost computer time, was over $100 million.

Trojan horse   A trojan horse is a program that looks like something else, but as soon as it is activated, its malevolent nature will quickly become apparent. Typical examples are programs that claim to be games or interesting utilities, which indeed may implement the claimed functions. However, they may execute differently and disastrously under certain circumstances. An early example was a program called EGABTR, which was described as providing a higher quality graphic display on IBM-PC compatible computers. However, as soon as the program is run, it proceeds to delete files and data from the hard disk. The Aids disk already mentioned on page 13 is another now classic example of the trojan horse, although interestingly it is often incorrectly described as the Aids 'Virus' - see below.

Trojan horse programs are extremely easy to write. In particular, trojan horse writers may use the natural curiosity of many computer users as the basis of their downfall. If a user finds a new command or file within a system, there is often a temptation to explore the new object directly, without reference to documentation or approval from system managers. For example, if a program called SEX suddenly appears in a computer system, there would be few users or computer managers who would not be sorely tempted to try the program out, or at least take a copy for later use. It would be an exceptional individual who would attempt to study the program *before* running it, or at least moving it to an isolated machine where any damage caused would be limited. It is for this reason amongst others that a strictly enforced policy of no unauthorised software is an extremely sensible one for organizations.

A minor variation on the theme of the trojan horse is the 'trapdoor'. Here, additional programs or instructions are built into a computer system in as discreet a fashion as possible. The extra code is intended to provide alternative facilities or access to the system. Consequently, trapdoors may be used by professional programmers to enable quick and easy access when a system has been developed, and indeed they may be of value in situations where they provide immediate and direct access when, for example, a computer system goes out of control and normal login methods are somehow inoperative.

A key attribute of the trapdoor is that it will almost invariably bypass system audit and command log facilities. In many cases, the presence of a trapdoor can only be detected by comparing actual processing demands with those formally registered and recorded by the system, and noting any significant discrepancy. This requires that the trapdoor should have been used several times in order to be highlighted as different from the normal minor variations in system load and capacity. Consequently, trapdoors can be very difficult to detect and deal with.

Logic bombs These are a major variation on the theme of the trojan horse. Logic bombs contain program code which remains dormant until a specific event or type of event occurs.

For example, an employee may be dismissed from an organization, and the absence of the employee's name on the payroll may be detected by a logic bomb inserted into a staff payroll program, or even an entirely different program in a separate part of the system.

Having detected that the employee is no longer on the payroll, the logic bomb can then proceed to 'detonate'. This may take the form of a wide-ranging and highly damaging data deletion activity.

Alternatively, the advent of a particular date may trigger some activities. April 1st and any Friday 13th seem to be popular choices in those cases which are documented. Logic bombs of this latter kind are often referred to as *time bombs*; but in reality they are simply logic bombs for which the logical trigger event is a date or time combination.

Logic bombs may be installed for blackmail purposes. A programmer inserts the logic bomb into the computer system, and demands payment to remove the bomb, or to prevent it from operating. The only sensible course of action in such instances is to inform the police.

An example of this threat was provided in July 1991, when programmers for a major US defense contractor discovered a logic bomb placed by an employee in a system used for developing missile programs. The logic bomb itself was intended to trigger on the day before a major public holiday, and proceed to delete important information and then erase itself. The employee had planned to resign from his post, and then demand large consultancy fees to repair the damage. The bomb was only discovered by accident - as is so often the case - when a colleague found he was unable to access certain files.

The problem for organizations is that logic bombs are often small programs and can be hidden very easily, sometimes in apparently unconnected parts of the system. Without the original source code, it can be extremely difficult to detect any additional code that has been written to implement a logic bomb, and indeed some assemblers or compilers actually include commands to make certain sections of the code invisible. These were originally intended to help minimise code complexity, but like any facility, are capable of being misused. Many commentators suggest that increasing numbers of disgruntled staff who are computer literate may turn to using malicious software programs, such as logic bombs, in order to try to harm their former employers.

Viruses   Perhaps the most famous category of automated threat is a combination of worm, logic bomb and trojan horse: the computer virus. Like worm programs, viruses can spread from machine to machine. Like the logic bomb, they can remain dormant until a certain trigger event occurs. Like the trojan horse, they can disguise themselves to appear innocuous, or even invisible to all but the most thorough investigator. Although they are not always the most damaging form of computer system threat, they appear to have received a disproportionate amount of publicity owing to their 'media appeal'.

As with their biological counterparts, computer viruses have a circular life-cycle consisting of four stages (figure 1): reproduction, transmission, infection and actuation. During the reproduction stage, a virus will attempt to replicate itself within an already infected system. Typically, the virus will attach itself to an uninfected program so that subsequent use of the newly-infected program can perpetuate the infestation process. During transmission, the virus will attempt to spread to another external system. This is where the virus will try to copy itself onto a floppy disk or other medium which is used for moving data or programs between machines. The infection stage is where the virus attempts to 'infiltrate' a program for the first time on the new target system. Viruses will typically attempt to attach themselves to other programs, but in certain

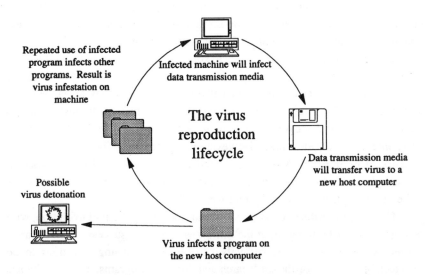

The virus reproduction lifecycle

Repeated use of infected program infects other programs. Result is virus infestation on machine

Infected machine will infect data transmission media

Data transmission media will transfer virus to a new host computer

Possible virus detonation

Virus infects a program on the new host computer

Figure 1: The four stages in the virus lifecycle

circumstances they will also target command procedures, batch files, parts of the operating system, or conceivably a simple data file.

The reproduction and infection cycle will continue with the numbers of viruses growing and spreading, until such time as the virus is eradicated in some fashion. Throughout this cycle, however, the virus can monitor its environment like a logic bomb, searching for an actuation trigger. These triggers are events or conditions which cause the virus to take supplementary steps that may be of a highly destructive nature.

However, there are certain practical constraints upon viruses which mean that it is difficult for them to be a general-purpose threat. A truly 'portable' virus cannot take advantage of necessarily system-specific features that could help hide it, unless it is a very advanced and complex program system in its own right. This in turn would render the virus more prone to detection owing to its physical size and much more extensive demands upon host system resources. The result is that viruses will normally be aimed at very specific machine environments, and consequently cannot exist outside that environment.

A mid-1992 estimate of micro-processor usage in computers indicated that chips manufactured by Intel Corporation are to be found in 100 million machines, more than five times its nearest competitor. The widespread utilization of these chips in IBM-compatible personal computers, coupled with the total absence of any meaningful protection mechanisms in the basic architecture of the computer, means that viruses targeted at IBM-compatible machines are numerous. In contrast, the more complex the host computer architecture, or the more unusual the installation of that machine type, the less common computer viruses will be for that environment.

The mechanisms used by viruses to spread are varied but in general require direct access to the system resources, in order to make modifications to memory or data stored on disks. Although network implementations are a perfectly viable means of facilitating virus spread, normal network administration and environment control measures are usually perfectly adequate to prevent wide-scale infection of a network. However, it is very easy for the server on a network to be infected by a virus, particularly during normal maintenance or repair tasks carried out by authorized staff. In theory, it is possible for a virus to be targeted at the network system itself.

The 'natural history' of viruses illustrates a clear pattern of evolution, with new generations building upon the attributes of earlier successes and failures. Current virus technology is perfectly capable of disguising infections to be undetectable by state-of-the-art 'search and destroy' programs, and even the use of verification programs could be subverted by a resident and active virus, which can be programmed to detonate if a virus detection package is used.

Following detection, eradication of a computer virus is a comparatively straightforward task in the vast majority of cases. As with medical complaints, the earlier the problem is detected, the greater the chance of a successful cure. Unfortunately, repairing damage done by a virus that has detonated can be a much more costly and time-consuming business. Consequently, by far the best approach for dealing with viruses is to try to ensure that they never get into a system in the first place. This requires a total ban on unauthorized software, such as games or pirated programs. Additionally, serious consideration should be given to banning import or export of data on disks to or from the organization.

The most unpleasant characteristics of viruses are firstly, that the damage which can result from a virus may be totally disproportionate to the size of the virus itself; and secondly that almost anyone could write a virus and release it into a system.

For example, the 16th March 1992 edition of the McGraw-Hill publication *International Business Week*, carried an article that described a problem at the Ignalina Nuclear Power Plant in Eastern Lithuania. In mid-January, monitoring computers reported that the first reactor was getting too hot owing to inadequate flushing with cooling water. If the problem was not addressed, the conditions were forming for another Chernobyl.

However, other non-computer-based sensors reported that all systems were running normally. Rather than shutting down the reactor, Sergei Slesarenko, the

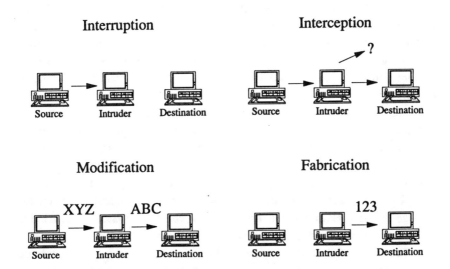

Figure 2: Threats to computer-based information systems

chief control-room engineer decided to reload the software into the monitoring computers, to try and clear up any glitches that had appeared. The reloading process took two hours, during which time the facilities for monitoring of the reactor were seriously constrained.

When the software had been reloaded, the problem appeared to go away. Yet the same symptoms came back a short time later in the shift, and again. Each time, the software had to be reloaded to cure the problem temporarily. About a week later, the cause was identified. A disgruntled employee had written a computer virus and implanted it into the software.

The results of a successful attack

If an attack of any kind on a computer-based information system is successful, there are four possible kinds of threat that can result (figure 2).

The first of these is *interruption*. This means that, following an attack on the system, some asset or resource that is supported, created or manipulated by the system becomes damaged or inaccessible for a possibly extended period. Typically, information normally available from a source cannot be communicated to the desired destination. Interruption of an information system in this way could be extremely damaging to the organization. Being unable to access customer information, or order processing information, or financial or credit details could have a dramatic effect on the business activities of the organization.

The second threat is *interception*. Here, someone from outside the organization can gain access to its information system in order to view the data that is being processed. In everyday terms, the nearest equivalent is the example of putting a 'tap' on a telephone line. Interception enables an outsider to acquire and perhaps make use of internal and possibly confidential data, to exploit for their own advantage.

The third category of threat that can occur following a successful attack is *modification* of the information. Here, an unauthorized party - who may be from inside the organization, as well as from outside - changes an asset or resource. A good example of this category is the 'salami attack' that has already been referred to on page 9. An alternative form of modification is to replace existing data with misleading or inaccurate data. A classic objective for teenage hackers is to try and break into a computer system which holds examination marks, and increase individual grades.

The fourth and final category of threat is *fabrication*. This is a more extreme form of modification where new data or transactions are entered into the information system. Typically, it would have value to the perpetrator as a means of directly inserting disinformation into an organization in order to produce substantial errors. However, fabricated information suffers from the drawback of being easy to identify unless it complies with all the relevant checking and verification details. These checks can be extremely wide-ranging, and may vary from a simplistic count of the expected number of characters stored in a file to a complex mathematical assessment of the patterns in number sequences. The result is that fabrication can be extremely difficult for someone to achieve, even if they have the benefit of inside information concerning what checks are applied.

Of the four categories, interception is perhaps the most dangerous for an organization, as it may be the least obvious - and hence more difficult to detect. This is because the organization can be losing information unwittingly over an extended period of time.

An example of interception occurred in a European university, where students studying electronics as part of their degrees decided to carry out some 'extra-curricular activity'. They built small devices that plugged into the back of computer terminals. These devices were built to look like small plugs similar to those normally found at the back of terminals, and so would pass all but the most detailed inspection.

However, inside the plugs were small dedicated computers that simply looked for password information moving to and from the terminal. As passwords were requested and transmitted, copies were taken and stored in the memory of the plug. At any time later, a student could retrieve the plug and decode the password information at leisure. This enabled the students to obtain many usernames and passwords, and hence gain almost unrestricted access to the computer systems.

The same method was used with breath-taking audacity by students to obtain the system manager's password. This occurred when the manager left an office door unlocked. This enabled a student to quickly slip into the office and attach the password-detecting plug onto the manager's terminal. Later, a similar lapse in security meant that another student was able to retrieve the plug and hence obtain the manager's password.

An alternative method of interception is based on the fact that many items of computer equipment actually 'broadcast' signals that correspond to the data being processed or displayed. The physical nature of the equipment is such that they transmit information in a manner that can be decoded, given the correct reception equipment.

The potential seriousness of this problem resulted in the development of TEMPEST, which stands for Transient Electro-Magnetic Pulse Emanation Standard. Specifically, TEMPEST is concerned with the amount of radiation a device may emit before compromising the information that it is processing. The most extreme example of decoding such emissions would, in theory, enable someone equipped with suitable electronics to reconstitute the signals generated by a VDU into a readable form. In practice, however, this method of interception remains unreliable and unworkable in most situations for three reasons.

- The equipment emitting the signals was not intended to broadcast information, and so the range of such transmissions is likely to be very limited.
- A variety of other equipment is also likely to be nearby, resulting in a 'swamping' of signals.
- The person monitoring the signals cannot control what information the computer operator looks at, so it will be a matter of luck to record useful data.

The example of the password-detecting plug could be categorised as a covert interception. If an interception is covert, this means that no traces are left which could facilitate detection of the interception. In the case of the password-detecting plug, no mechanism existed for the system or users to check if their password was being recorded by this device. The only way in which the interception could be detected would be by spotting the plug at the back of the terminal, or after the authorized user's password had been used by someone else.

The alternative to covert interception is overt interception. Here, the interception occurs in a manner which can be detected, for example using signal strengths or delays.

In some secure computer systems, the time taken for information to move between devices - say from computer to terminal and back - is measured very precisely. If the time delay changes, there is a high probability that the communications channel is no longer secure. Similarly, if the communications channel is broken for any period of time, there is again the possibility that the security of the channel has been compromised.

The targets of information system attack

There are three specific entities or components of an information system that may be subject to attack: hardware, software and the data itself.

The hardware or physical devices are easily identified, and correspondingly attack procedures may be easier to identify. There are many near-apocryphal tales of the onslaughts on computers, including floods, burning, stabbings, shooting, theft, bombing, shorting by paper clips, drowning in coffee, and so on. Theft and destruction of this kind represent the primary risks for most items of hardware. As a result, major systems of any measurable value should be kept isolated in a controlled environment.

However, with increasing standardization of technology, the actual make of hardware that forms the foundation of the system may become less important. In theory, it should be possible for any hardware failures to be accommodated or a new system reconstructed fairly quickly once replacement equipment is obtained, so long as three preconditions are met:

- The functional characteristics of the system are known and can be replicated or restored.
- A suitably strict regime of backups has been carried out.
- Any innovations or modifications to the system have been fully and methodically documented.

Unfortunately, the effort required to provide the reconstruction facility can be costly in terms of time and resources needed. As a result, some organizations will be tempted to neglect this aspect of information system protection.

An alternative approach is to off-load full responsibility for information systems to an external organization. This concept, known as Facilities Management or FM, does have disadvantages, however, and will be discussed in more detail later.

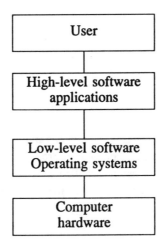

Figure 3: Simple representation of computer system components

Given the comparative ease with which hardware can be replaced - assuming there has been full and adequate management and administration of the original hardware - we can conclude that hardware on its own should be of little value *per se*. More important should be the software and data, in a variety of forms, which represents the real key to obtaining value from the physical hardware, and furthermore, will form the operational and functional heart of the information system.

Software may be loosely divided into the applications and environmental tools (operating systems and packages or programs); and operational data and information. It is a common convention to refer to operating systems and similar tools as low-level software (see figure 3), while application packages and major programs are considered to be high-level software.

In general, the lower the level of the software within the system, the more difficult it is to access and modify it in any way without the effects becoming apparent very rapidly. This is because the construction of low-level software - which must have an intrinsic relationship to the hardware - is normally extremely complex.

Low-level software, such as an operating system, must be optimised for providing the maximum speed and range of functions, but with minimum use of resources and minimum number of errors. These constraints make very skilful programming mandatory. Any unskilled modification to low-level software is therefore very likely to produce dramatic and obvious variations in system performance.

By contrast, high-level software such as word-processors or database programs can often be modified much more easily and subtly. These programs are still very complex, but the much larger scale means that even quite significant changes can be 'hidden' from the end users. This property of high-level software is used all the time by software developers when they issue a new version of a package that is 'compatible' with earlier versions - even if the actual implementation is totally different. Some software developers go to great lengths to ensure that a new version of some software is visually unaltered.

The possibility of unexplained interactions and poorly understood structures can - over the course of time - combine to produce unpleasant effects in software. At first inspection, a newly installed package may appear to be acceptable, but before long it will begin to reveal the presence of bugs - some of them quite serious.

Some users of computer systems will tend to blame themselves for difficulties in the operation of the software, due to the seeming infallibility of computers. Rather than addressing problems in the software, they may tend to address non-existent problems in users operating procedures. The result may be that user inexperience or software complexity will combine in a fashion that encourages users to believe that all programs will have bugs in them. This in turn means that users will be more likely to tolerate strange or unpredictable behaviour.

The absence of a software tool can be quickly and easily detected, but modifications to an existing tool may be much more difficult to identify. Often, the modification is such that it enables the software to do something *in addition to* the tasks performed originally, and therefore normal usage of the original functions alone is unlikely to reveal any discrepancies unless there is accidental or deliberate interference. The modifications may be particularly difficult to detect if they can only be activated in the presence of a particular logical condition; this concept forms the foundation of the 'logic bomb' referred to earlier.

Administration of data is the main purpose of an information system. The system will be devoted to the appropriate accumulation, alteration and assignment of data, according to requirements. As is already well understood, this data can represent a resource of fundamental value to the organization. If data can be presented or accessed in a form suitable for interpretation by an authorized user, there is a high degree of probability that the data can also be read by an unauthorized user, once access controls have been bypassed.

In other words, data has a greater general value than the hardware or software that comprises an information system. Furthermore, the value itself will tend to vary according to time, in that data obtained at various stages during its collection may be of low or high value, according to its accuracy and relevance as time passes. Conversely, out-of-date data is clearly of reduced value.

Modification, poor availability, or excessive inaccuracy or unreliability, can all directly and significantly influence the value of data to an organization and its activities.

The CIA model

Having identified typical threats that computer systems may be subjected to, and the resulting categories of damage that can occur, we must now turn to the problem of preventing the threats. A large number of mechanisms may be implemented in a computer system to provide security, but it is also important to have a framework or model within which to direct the activities of securing the system.

The most basic of computer security concepts are currently implemented using the so-called CIA model. This rather appropriate acronym stands for Confidentiality, Integrity and Availability, and epitomises the primary objectives in trying to secure a computer-based information system. The objective for most computer security specialists is to analyze the target system with a view to ensuring satisfactory compliance with these three goals. The CIA concepts are widely regarded as representing the basic properties that a computer-based information system should have if it is to be described as supporting computer security.

Confidentiality

A major factor in the value of many objects is the secrecy of the object. Typical examples would include engineering designs, student examination papers, agricultural produce estimates, financial plans and accounts, and so on. Accordingly, such objects should be protected from disclosure to unauthorized personnel.

Confidentiality refers to the need to ensure that items from within the computer system are not disseminated beyond certain bounds. Exactly what constitutes these bounds is more difficult to define, and will vary according to the object and the circumstances. Clearly, only authorized persons should have access to restricted data.

However, current computer technology allows remote and indirect access to data from other computer systems. In such a case, it is possible for a computer to be initiating the access request, and computers cannot be authorized persons. There may be different levels of confidentiality for different items of data, and some of these levels may vary depending upon the context of a specific enquiry.

Integrity

The integrity of the computer-based information system relates to the preservation of the actual value of the material that is stored or processed. If the data is in any way unreliable, inaccurate or incomplete, then at best it is useless, and at worst it may be detrimental to the continued success of the organization. Integrity may be viewed as having several subtle nuances of meaning, including a reference to the preservation of an object against unauthorized change.

On a larger scale, the integrity of the entire computer-based information system is of importance in that it must preserve the value of all its components, in particular with respect to the file objects and security functions. A frequently successful approach to take in order to breach system security is first to exploit weaknesses in the security mechanisms themselves.

Integrity refers to the need to ensure that data stored within a computer system is correct and is kept as complete as is minimally necessary for the desired purpose. The need for correctness is understandable, but the completeness requirement may not be so obvious. A simple example might be found in a mailing list stored on computer. Using a computer to send out mail by generating address labels, for example to deliver to a Ms Smith at 32, The Street, Anytown, may well result in the post being delivered to the correct location.

However, if Ms Smith is one of a family which includes several daughters, then there is the possibility of ambiguity concerning the intended recipient of the post. In this situation, more data is needed to ensure that the post is delivered to the correct person. Failing that, the delivery could be delayed or even directed to the wrong person.

Nevertheless, it would be excessive to store more data than is necessary to achieve the stated purpose. For example, if the computer system is to be used simply to store mailing addresses, there should be no need for it to store age, financial or vehicle ownership details for that person.

If a computer system is to be used for storing or processing data, it is preferable that the storage should be as accurate as possible, in order to reflect the correct, current status of the data. Quite apart from any data protection restrictions, or the space and cost overhead for storing otherwise irrelevant data, the additional material will inevitably delay the processing of database queries and transactions.

Availability

For a computer-based information system to be of continuing value, it must be able to offer the desired access, upon demand, to authorized users. It may be that the system has stored a large quantity of valuable data, but unless the users can access that material, the system is of minimal value. The lack of availability is sometimes referred to as denial of service, although this may then be confused with the related issue of specifically preventing an otherwise authorized user from performing a particular task or accessing some specific material.

Availability is the need for a computer system to provide a meaningful response to an authorized user upon request and without delay, or to react promptly and correctly in response to instructions from the user.

As an example, it may safely be assumed that most airline pilots and passengers would be less than happy at being carried in an aircraft that was controlled by computer systems and for which there was a minimum of a thirty-second delay before any commands would be obeyed by the aircraft. Similarly, shops and businesses would not be quick to adopt and utilize a credit card referral system for which every check of a credit card prior to a purchase took ten minutes.

The nature of people

While very helpful at identifying threats, the CIA concept does have certain limitations. Its use can result in an emphasis on technology to provide the required solutions. This may be because system specialists apply CIA by studying how a system can be attacked. In order to provide suggestions on how to attack a system, the specialists will have a great deal of technical expertise. But the end result could be a technical approach to the identification of threats, and any subsequent implementation of 'solutions'.

But people are the real key players and can subvert any technological solution. It is understandable if a technological approach will try to exclude the unpredictability and inconsistency of people. But this minimises the opportunity for consideration of the primary source and cause of threats to information systems.

Unfortunately, of the many users of an information system, not all will work in a productive way. Given the opportunity and appropriate circumstances, most people will want to improve their situation. In some cases, personal gain may only be achieved by carrying out actions that would not otherwise be contemplated. The decision on whether or not to carry out their actions will largely depend upon the perceived balance or 'pay-off' between the gains and risks.

The issue is complicated by the fact that the measure of what constitutes tolerable risk varies from person to person and situation to situation. Furthermore, that interpretation is not constant or predictable; it will vary with the changing circumstances of the individual. Desperate people are notoriously prone to doing desperate things that they would not otherwise contemplate.

Thus actions may be performed by individuals or groups in the full knowledge that they are unlawful, or unethical, or in some way contrary to conventional standards. Nevertheless, the final 'reward' may be thought to be sufficient incentive.

As a simple example, although the speed limits on roads should be well-known, many drivers will exceed the limit - perhaps by a significant margin - if they believe they will not suffer from their actions. Their objective is to get to their destination more quickly. The advantages of this are presumably thought to outweigh the risk of having a serious accident, or being caught for speeding. Technology is then wilfully misapplied to enable an individual to perform an unlawful act.

There are many other examples where technology could be deliberately misapplied for dubious purposes. However, it is the recognition of an alternative way in which the technology can be applied that lies at the heart of the particular difficulty of systems security.

Summary

In this chapter, we have considered the basic concepts of computer security. We have looked at the natural, accidental and deliberate problems, and highlighted some the computer-specific threats that can be applied to systems.

In general terms, the results of a particular threat can be described according to four classifications: interruption, interception, modification and fabrication. A model may be used to implement mechanisms which attempt to deal with these threats.

However, it is suggested that the main emphasis of computer security is often - incorrectly - upon the technology, and specifically the hardware of the system. A wider perspective on the current nature of computer systems and the circumstances in which they are installed indicates that we should instead place much greater emphasis upon two alternative areas: the data itself and the data users.

Before we can reach that point, however, we need to look more closely at the way organizations become dependent upon technology, and how systems may be more securely designed.

2 The technology trap

- **The emphasis on technology**
- **The technology trap**
- **Why the technology trap is perpetuated**
- **The technician as manager**
- **Summary**

An implicit theme running through the chapter on basic concepts is the recognition that technology provides the opportunity for great harm as well as great good for organizations. It is easy to think of examples where items of otherwise benign technology have been misunderstood, misapplied, or misused with serious consequences.

The task of dealing with computer security is made more difficult by the uncontrolled acceptance of technology. Many organizations still consider that use of computer technology will automatically improve productivity or solve administrative difficulties. In the absence of careful planning, such an optimistic viewpoint cannot be sustained. Furthermore, if utilization of technology has not been carefully planned, it is also unlikely that the security aspects of technology will have been sufficiently considered.

But businesses are not alone in their optimistic view of technology. For almost all levels of education in the developed world, some form of computer studies are a mandatory component. Unfortunately, in teaching students about computers, important security implications of information technology may be neglected.

We can refer to these difficulties of perspective as the 'technology trap'. The value of recognising this concept is that it helps us in our efforts to understand more about the threats to computer security.

The emphasis on technology

An interesting paradox of information technology is that although computers are of greatest value when used for processing of information, the perception of computers tends to emphasise the technological issues rather than the way in which the machines and systems may be applied to problems.

Instead of considering what the objectives of an information system are, or should be, technological emphasis encourages consideration only of what

29

objectives are possible in view of the available computer technology. The result is that solutions are often tailored more according to technological feasibility rather than application and objective desirability.

Evidence that there is undue emphasis on technology is not hard to find, once the issue has been identified. One example concerns the extensive training that users need before they can use many computer applications. Extra guidance is required to learn the new system, because it may not be intuitive for the user to understand how the computer system models the desired task. This is despite the fact that intuition is increasingly widely recognised as an important attribute of systems.

The importance of intuition for improving ease-of-use is underlined by advice given in the IBM Common User Access (CUA) Advanced Interface Design Guide:

> *'When you use metaphors that are familiar and real-world based, users can transfer previous knowledge of their work environment to your application interface. You must be careful in choosing a metaphor to make sure the metaphor meets the expectations users have because of their real-world experience.'*

CUA is part of IBM's System Application Architecture, SAA. SAA represents an attempt to standardize the software development process. The objective of CUA is to give applications a similar look and feel, irrespective of what computer or software environment is being used. Thus if a particular keypress calls up a help function in one CUA-compliant package, it should do so in all CUA-compliant packages.

The CUA principles are undoubtedly helpful in that once the user has learnt how to use a CUA-compliant application, other CUA-compliant applications should be much easier to learn. But this does not mean that system will be any easier for a user to comprehend.

An everyday example of the objectives of CUA concerns the Graphic User Interface or GUI. Despite the claim of providing a 'desk-top' on a screen, GUIs offer only a very crude approximation to an office environment. This results in some strange techniques for performing tasks, such as the use of a mouse to open or close windows. While easy to use, the mouse is not a metaphor for any equivalent in the real world.

Further evidence for the emphasis on technology can be found in training courses, and textbooks and other documentation. In many of these sources, the discussion of information systems, and ultimately the understanding of issues associated with the systems, seems to be apportioned according to a ratio of approximately 90:10. This suggests that in any collection of computer related material, some 90% will concentrate upon technology issues, and how to make the technology perform particular tasks.

By contrast, only 10% of the material addresses the issue of *why* tasks need to be performed, or what the implications will be for users or organizations that employ computers in handling tasks. The ratio was identified by the simple technique of the author inspecting 100 books which discuss various aspects of information technology, and keeping a page count. While clearly a rough measurement, it does provide further evidence of the observed emphasis on technology.

This emphasis can influence the way that information system issues are considered. For example, the developers and producers of computer system tools or training materials often make at least one fundamental assumption: the fact that you have purchased the tool means that you are already satisfied as to its suitability for the desired task. In other words, you know exactly what you want to use it for, and also how it will function within your organization. Very rarely will the instructions for the tool deal with the effect of the application on the user's overall organizational position, let alone the implications of computerisation for departments and upon organizational strategy. It is very rare for the question to be asked: 'Why is a computer system required anyway, and what effect will the system have upon the organization?'.

In the absence of a wide understanding of the issues, people dealing with information technology may be tempted to focus on the components of the problem that are comparatively well understood. This may be due to the desire to simplify the issues as much as possible. Even if the overall difficulty is not solved, at least the technical component of the problem has been addressed. The remainder of the matter then becomes someone else's responsibility. In effect, emphasis on technology may be used as a life-raft to escape from part of the obligation.

More specifically, emphasis on technology has implications for computer security. A quick review of state-of-the-art computer security mechanisms confirms the view that a predominantly technology-orientated perspective is taken when making provision for the necessary protection.

Computer security is usually provided using software or hardware technology. For example, data may be protected using one or more of the following techniques:

It may be disguised so that anyone gaining access to it is unable to interpret it. The disguise may be implemented using encryption mechanisms such as the Data Encryption Standard (DES).

- It may be hidden. Access is strictly limited to those who have appropriate and verifiable authority. Access control mechanisms include passwords and authorized user lists.
- It may be validated. This prevents data modification or fabrication from occurring either deliberately or by accident. Validation may be implemented using data labels or attributes, checksum or data integrity calculations. These supplement the original data.

Using such methods, a security specialist can offer a substantial level of data protection. The main distinction between programs and data is one of interpretation, and so similar mechanisms could be utilized for protection of software.

Protection of hardware may be achieved by a number of mechanisms. Apart from mechanical locks on doors and the actual system boxes, there are a variety of technological devices that are intended to prevent unauthorized use, theft or damage of the hardware.

These include expansion units to provide access control, plug-in modules or 'dongles' that uniquely code some aspect of the system, 'trembler' switches to detect excessive motion such as occurs when the computer is being moved, and so on.

It may be that a number of methods are implemented in parallel or sequence, to cross-check each other and further improve the integrity of the system. However, this does not alter our observation that, in many cases, difficulties which can arise from the introduction, use and subsequent misuse of technology are often solved by applying yet more technology.

Although in many cases there are perfectly adequate non-computer-based mechanisms for providing computer security, it seems that a mindset has developed where security threats arising from technology are often assumed to require technical answers. The assumption stems from the widely-held belief in the benefits of technology, and the associated emphasis on technological solutions.

The technology trap

We are now in a position to identify a label for difficulties which can result from emphasis upon technology. The technology trap may be defined as being the situation that occurs when technology is introduced into problem situations by technical staff within organizations, without complete consideration of the implications.

If the implications are not understood, the organization cannot be certain that adoption of computer technology is appropriate for their requirements.

Furthermore, the task of providing security for the computer-based information system is made more difficult for a similar reason.

It is easy for individuals and organizations to fall into the technology trap, because the issues are so insidious and simple, particularly at the beginning. For example, an organization might begin by procuring a single word-processor to experiment with. The facilities of the machine are used more and more by increasing numbers of staff. Demands for more machines means that numbers begin to multiply. Users begin to share files, and this requires the development of a filing and cross-referencing system.

Before long, demands for upgrading and sharing of applications and data compel the introduction of a network, and following that comes the need for some sort of coherent strategy for dealing with the diverse technologies and minor incompatibilities that have suddenly been identified within different departments, and so on.

Personal computers are symbolic examples of causes of the technology trap, in that they are cheap enough to be hidden within the petty cash figures of departmental budgets, and yet powerful enough to wreck the information movements of the organization if misused.

Implications of the technology trap

There are some application areas where computer technology can be seen to have a measurable benefit - normally where the systems will be used almost exclusively to perform repetitive or detailed tasks rapidly, or with extreme precision on large quantities of data. Successful examples tend to focus upon large-scale database requirements, such as banks issuing regular statements of account to all their customers.

However, the number of such easily-understood categories of applications are perhaps rather rare. One can intuitively appreciate that if a large amount of data is to be manipulated using extremely repetitive sequences, then it makes sense to apply a tool that is efficient at performing continual tasks on large quantities of information. Many users can quickly grasp the principles of database tools through the helpful analogy of the filing cabinet used for storing and cross-referencing data.

In order to help users overcome any difficulties with understanding an operational paradigm, greater emphasis in manuals or courses will be devoted to explaining *exactly* how a particular tool is used. This means that material on word-processing or Computer Aided Design (CAD) is more likely to address the utilization of the tools *irrespective* of the specific environment, rather than how the tools operate within, and influence the ongoing nature of, the working environment.

But if organizations do not really understand their information system, it is difficult to measure its value, its contribution, and also the difficulties that could result following computer system failure.

If the initial adoption of technology is on a small scale, or for a highly specific function, such as replacing a typewriter with a dedicated word-processing system, or a filing cabinet with a database, then the organizational implications may be minimal for both the short and medium term. But a major advantage of the computerised information system is that it can provide much longer term storage facilities.

This has two significant implications. Firstly, items of data, even if they appear to be simple collections of memos or short documents, are being recorded. Collected data can become very valuable. For example, a set of data may enable recognition of trends or support faster access to more comprehensive accounting information. When data is processed on a large scale, it can become information, and will be a valuable resource in its own right. Before long, the organization may come to depend upon the resource, which therefore must be managed.

Secondly, as the importance of this information resource grows, a need develops for providing a consistent structuring mechanism. There must be a way to optimise the organization of the data in order to minimise wastage and make usage straightforward. Data, and any information derived from it, should be accessible by those who are authorized to do so. An on-going structure development and evaluation process should therefore be carried out to ensure that such access can be provided.

In order to understand the implications of this, we must reconsider what is meant by an 'information system'. Certainly it would appear to be an important concept, if only when measured by the number of organizations, both businesses and in academia, that now refer to an information systems department in preference to the title of computer systems, services or science. More than one professional body has changed its name to reflect the move away from computing and technology, and more towards information and systems and engineering.

A key point in the definition of an information system, and hopefully within any implementation of what is claimed to be an information system, is the importance of people. Only now is the importance of this factor becoming recognised more widely. Without such recognition, the technology trap causes more problems because while organizations *want* information systems, they are *getting* computer technology.

In addition, the failure to address social aspects makes it extremely difficult to modify systems to accommodate the subsequent environmental changes which naturally and inevitably occur. Examples include the implementation of new business strategies, modified performance targets, and even the presence or absence of skills following staff turnover.

Thus, while the technicians have a steady job, maintaining and 'fine-tuning' their 'information systems', they have less time for the business requirements of the rest of the organization. Under such circumstances, it is not surprising if organizations are disappointed by the unfulfilled promise of computers, and may be frustrated at what is deemed to be irrelevant or overly-complex technology.

It is wrong to assume that the introduction of even the simplest form of computer technology cannot ultimately have a profound influence upon the organization. Nor can these influences be confined within the boundaries of the organization. This is because of the rapid rate at which the effects of computerisation spread beyond the bounds of the organization, using data communication networks or open systems.

Open systems

Open systems is a concept that refers to the interconnection of multiple computer systems of different types. Open systems provide facilities to access and exchange data or resources between different applications on the various machines.

The objective that lies behind implementing open systems is to provide a mechanism for information of various kinds to move to and from the controlled domain, possibly through links to other organizations. An implication of this is that organizations may lose some control over their information resources for some of the time. This has profound implications for the organization.

An information system may be constructed in part or in whole using networking technology. This means that users can gain access to resources or facilities on an individual or shared basis at different locations.

As a simple example, most computer-based information systems that support multiple users will provide a centralised processing resource to support large database storage, or to allow use of an expensive but high-quality typesetting system.

In an attempt to provide simple and effective exchange of data between users and computer systems, an extremely intricate collection of technology disciplines must be applied to the problem. Basic electronics skills are necessary to implement the wiring between machines, and increasingly there is a need for more advanced physics to be applied to the problem of installing high-speed and high-capacity microwave or fibre-optic cable links. The physical connections must be monitored and controlled by the operating system software

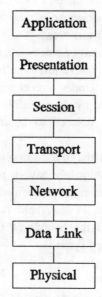

Figure 4: The OSI model

within the computer. Communication facilities and services must be provided to applications that are running on the machine. These services must be easy for users to work with. Given the various levels of complexity, it is highly desirable to adopt a simplifying model that may be used to represent the various components of the systems, and their potential interactions.

For computer networks, the model is the International Standards Organization (ISO) seven-layer model for Open Systems Interconnection (OSI), as shown in figure 4. Each of the layers represents a specific part of the problem. For example, the lowest layer addresses the physical issues such as wiring and electronic representation of data. The highest layer is concerned with the way in which programs and applications can use the communication facilities. Use of this model enables the developers to concentrate on specific areas such as ensuring successful transmission of the data, or converting it to different forms; these can all be considered in isolation from the other topics.

Since the main objective of development work of this kind is to promote easier and more useful communications facilities, it is not surprising if provision of security mechanisms for protection purposes appears to play a comparatively small role in the overall treatment. This is because security is often seen as interfering with tasks, and constraining the range of tasks that may be performed. Both of these limitations are extremely undesirable in computer networks.

Certainly, techniques such as data encryption and passwords and other security measures do have a place within the communications model. Other security mechanisms will be incorporated, particularly into the lower layers, in order to provide error detection and correction facilities. However, by delegating consideration of such issues to a specific part of the model, it may be difficult to ensure that security considerations are addressed *throughout* the open system development and implementation process.

In order to see why this issue represents a difficulty in data communications, we must introduce the idea of an 'access contender'. This is defined as an individual user or even a computer system resource that, for some reason, seeks to gain access to one or more other resources which are provided within the computer system domain.

Among other things, the desired functional characteristics of the information system as a whole will be used to develop the specification for the access control criteria. These are tests which must be performed to check the identity and authorization of the access contender. If the access contender is able to justify the request for resources, and complies with the well-understood and clearly defined set of criteria, then access is granted and the access contender will become an authorized user of the computer system resource.

But if the criteria are defined and implemented within only a limited part of the system model, because of the simplification process, then true access control may not apply throughout the entire system. Accordingly, having gained access via the necessary sections of the model, many other levels of access may be obtained by the access contender with much less difficulty, because one level of authorization has already been achieved.

In practice this does not pose a great difficulty for information systems where there is capacity for extremely thorough access criteria implementations. However, other systems, and particularly those which incorporate any small computers such as personal computers or certain types of workstations, do not necessarily have the capability to support such stringent checking. This weakness may be exploited to provide a route by which an access contender may obtain admission without necessarily having met all of the desired access criteria.

For example, the lack of inherent access control in most personal computers means that an access contender can very easily gain absolute control of the machine. This would be achieved by using a standard operating system disk to start the computer in a known state, without loading special software or performing specialised initialization activities. The result of this could be that some security mechanisms would have been bypassed. Following access in this way, further control may be gained over the physical implementation of data communications outside the machine which is provided by a combination of hardware and software. Since personal computer users can have almost unrestricted access to machine components, there is always the possibility that they are in a position to *modify* the configuration of that combination with only a small amount of technical knowledge.

It is extremely difficult to provide sufficiently rigorous access control mechanisms on personal computers. The basic architecture is now over a decade old, and as such was not designed with state-of-the-art security mechanisms in mind. Furthermore, the original personal computer designed by IBM was not expected to be success that it turned out to be, and the intended market for the machine was not thought to require substantial security provisions.

Today, the nature of the operating systems and hardware constraints mean that most applications tend to utilize all system resources to their maximum, and any changes away from a standard system configuration, such as access control mechanisms, can often result in a cumulative effect of conflict and subsequent system failure.

Returning to the open systems discussion, workable implementations of data communication tools are heavily dependent upon access and resource control. This is because mechanisms must be provided which allow multiple users to utilize a variety of resources, without coming into conflict with any of the other users or their tasks.

The extreme complexity of access and resource control implementation contrasts noticeably with the overall objectives of providing simple, easy-to-use, fast and efficient communications with minimum delay, as these represent organizational performance requirements.

This complexity is caused by the intricacy of network definitions and standards, as well as the need for verification and validation of transmissions. As with access to personal computer technology, a network access contender who succeeds in gaining entry to a communications system may, in theory, be in a position to misuse the resources by intercepting, fabricating or monitoring transmissions.

Another major area of threat for the security of networks concerns the administration and management of the network itself. It is in this example that some of the disadvantages of the technology trap start to manifest themselves. At first, technology appears to offer great benefits at minimal cost. But as the systems expand, administration and maintenance become major activities. Difficulties start to arise with minor incompatibilities between implementations, which *must* be corrected. As more technology is added, so the problems and their implications extend.

For example, in open systems there is continual movement and updating of information. One of the greatest advantages of networks is that they enable the sharing and storage of much larger quantities of data, often on a centralised server. Implementation of such systems usually aims at producing an environment where users can perform their tasks without having to worry about the functional data communication activities that are taking place in the background. An important part of these activities is ensuring that full and adequate backups of information are taken from the network environment. Someone must take the responsibility for ensuring that regular data backups are taken and, furthermore, that the network service facilities continue to function at optimum levels of performance.

In some systems, users may organise their work such that most data is stored on their own local workstation, but in other situations users may have no choice but to use a central server facility. Indeed, this may even be enforced through the use of 'diskless' workstations. There are advantages to this, for example it prevents users from using unauthorized software or data, and also stops people copying data onto removable media.

However, if there is a choice, consideration should be given to whether users should perform the backup of their own data, or whether the system operators should perform the task, or a combination of the two. Clearly if both parties are responsible for backup, the system is simultaneously safer and more open to weakness: it is less likely that information will be lost by accident, but more people have greater access to that data.

There is a need to develop and state a policy which defines what is required and expected of all people involved. The frequency of backups must also be satisfactory to all concerned. A weekly backup may not be sufficient for some users, who may then be tempted to perform more regular backups themselves. This in turn may be a security weakness with regard to the storage of the backup disks.

As a final point, one case may help to encourage users to perform backups. A US government employee working in El Salvador managed to lose all the data on the hard disk of a PC. His backup schedule had suffered from neglect, and it appeared that much of the information was lost. Unfortunately, his colleagues were 'freedom fighters' with a poor understanding of disk technology and reliability. Their view was that if the information was not made available - quickly - they would shoot him. Fortunately, the hapless individual knew of an experienced hardware engineer who was able to restore the data, and save his life.

Why the technology trap is perpetuated

Once the technology trap is in place, there is rarely an opportunity to change the situation without considerable upheaval. Few technicians see any need to change the nature of their speciality. They continue to study the new technology introduced by manufacturers, so that it can be introduced into the organization at the earliest opportunity.

This is despite the observation that for many users, a simple desk-top computer with a reasonably-sized hard disk (probably no more that 60MB in capacity) is likely to fulfil their needs for the foreseeable future. A more powerful machine would not be used for processing larger quantities of data, but for providing greater variety and optimum performance in the processing tasks themselves. If there is a need for additional data capacity, this could be provided using networking technology to larger file-server or even mini- or mainframe systems. We are reaching the point at which desk-top machines can now process more data than any one individual can easily comprehend. Larger quantities of data would have to be summarised or compressed anyway.

Another reason for the perpetuation is due to the way in which some systems are derived from more dated technologies. A primary example can be found in the personal computer environment, where IBM-compatible PCs are constrained by the DOS operating system which must still assume a minimal hardware configuration and which therefore cannot take advantage of the considerably more advanced technology available today.

Several other factors combine to encourage the perpetuation of the trap. For example, it may be suggested that managers of organizations cannot and should not turn their attention to technical matters, because it will inevitably detract from the quality of their work and attention to other details. Accordingly, consideration of technical details is a task that will be delegated to those individuals who are better trained to deal with such matters. Some technical staff may be happy for this to happen because they gain a degree of control and influence over the organization, if not immediately, then at some time in the future.

Learning to use technology

One of the most obvious reasons for the perpetuation of the technology trap is demonstrated by the way in which novices are introduced to computer systems. For almost any computer system or training course, the first things to be studied are the basic terms, and then how to switch the machine on, and how to give it commands. In essence, this is an overview of how to activate and direct the machine.

More detail is given in the form of the commands or directives used for controlling the computer. The material may be divided into two streams which reflect the purpose of the commands. Firstly, there are simple administrative functions that all users would be expected to perform at some time, such as copying or editing data files. Secondly, there are more advanced or user-specific applications that are only of relevance or interest to certain users. These might include spreadsheets, CAD tools, financial and accounting maintenance packages, and so on.

After the basics have been introduced, the user is taught how to start and use specific applications, depending on the main purpose for which the machine was bought. Alternatively, they might be encouraged to write their own computer programs. From the very beginning, the new user is being trained to consider the computer system and its applications from a technical perspective.

In most cases, the instructions for the package explain the basic activities, such as text entry for word-processors or number entry for spreadsheets. Then more advanced functions are introduced, such as paragraph handling, or use of formulae for manipulating data. Thereafter, various other detailed and specific options are introduced, for example 'macro' programming or how to use special features. Throughout, there will be simple but often contrived examples which are intended to show how the functions might be used in more complex situations. The emphasis will be on introducing the user to an application 'tool-kit', which they can then use as they want.

Similarly, programming manuals will have a highly techno-specific emphasis. Many provide only the most trivial of samples for the novice to practice with. It is very rare for an on-going and substantial application to be developed and constructed throughout a book; although this is perhaps understandable given that the book would then appeal only to readers interested in that particular application.

Most manuals begin by introducing a simple example of code, typically something that will print a welcoming message onto the computer screen. This is then analyzed to identify the key features. Alternative or better ways of achieving the same results are introduced, then more functions to perform more tasks. The process continues until the user knows how to program the computer using that particular tool. Here again the objective is to provide a 'tool-kit' that users can apply in any way they wish. In this way the emphasis on technology continues.

Few programming manuals address the issues of Systems Analysis and Design (SAD) in any detail. These are software engineering principles or guidelines which attempt to describe how a computer system may be designed such that it can be applied to a particular problem. We will return to SAD in a later chapter, but for the moment the significance of SAD is that for all but the simplest of computing problems, a great deal of thought should be given to how the problem and its solution are constructed.

Thus technical skills may be acquired by individuals pursuing their own studies in a self-taught manner, or from courses that tend to overlook social and managerial issues. The focus upon technology contrasts with the neglect of non-technological considerations, such as human-human interaction as facilitated by technology, or the implications of technology upon organizations and business functions. Furthermore, it inhibits the move away from viewing systemic issues as simple technological matters towards a more realistic and useful perspective.

The consequence is that many an organization, and indeed society, has a pool of capable but extremely specialised staff, who naturally exclude all but the most technical of considerations. These people have the responsibility of supplying a system to solve a problem, as identified by business managers. The result is a 'pseudo-information system' which may actually be a non-solution. This is because such systems rarely meet the ideals of those who must use them, and in the long term are unlikely to prove cost-effective.

Having completed a course on programming, or mastered the use of a particular package, the student may be an expert on the technological aspects of the system. But in learning to use the technology, emphasis will have been almost exclusively upon the technology. The result can be that the user is equipped with a package of inappropriate and incomplete skills and perceptions.

The technician as manager

Although the technology trap is, as its name suggests, founded in technology, its effects will eventually start to become noticeable in the social and administrative environment. In particular, it may constrain the options of those who specialise in computers.

Increasing levels of expertise are now being found within, or at least are available to, organizations. This means that there are greater numbers of computer-literate people who are in a position to reach senior and more responsible positions. Rather than concentrating exclusively upon day-to-day operational tasks and functions, such people will be starting to take part in more administrative duties, such as divisional or directorial responsibility.

However, owing to their background and career paths within the organization, many of these people will have had minimal exposure to the non-technical aspects of the organization. Staff who are highly competent at handling technical issues may be much less comfortable when dealing with other matters. Originally, they could concentrate exclusively on technology matters, for example by keeping up to date with the latest developments.

But promotion to management roles requires that people take responsibility for organizational matters such as development teams or business profit centres. In particular, they must demonstrate an understanding of business issues through their decision-making. Without these skills, technicians can experience great difficulty in finding and filling senior posts. For many computer specialists, their duties focus upon the development, installation or operation of systems for other people to use. They are more concerned with ensuring that a word-processor is operational, than with *how* and *why* it is used in a business. The result is that for many computer people, the pinnacle of their career may be as the topmost manager, or at best director, of the computer or information services department within the organization.

The difficulty for computer people seeking career advancement is that a training strategy which culminates in an extremely competent and experienced IT director is *not* necessarily an optimal route for someone who wishes to progress into non-IT-specific directorship.

As an experiment, a number of the leading computer firms in the UK were contacted to obtain personnel profile information about the senior staff. This information is widely available, and often provided with press releases following the appointment of a new executive. It is interesting to note that for many of those Information Technology companies, some of them major, almost all of the senior managers and executives are from sales and administrative backgrounds rather than computer engineering or programming. The exceptions are some organizations that are US-based, and which were founded by technical specialists who had a 'vision' of a new company. However, even then, the makeup of the senior management teams is predominantly from sales or administration.

The result of the technology trap, in this case, is that computer staff may become increasingly frustrated at their inability to advance. Even if they are promoted to higher levels, they may feel that they never quite 'fit in' with their colleagues, owing to a different perspective on issues.

One suggestion for dealing with the quandary is the so-called 'hybrid manager'. This is defined as someone who combines knowledge of information technology with business expertise. While it may be possible to train individuals specifically for this role in the future, perhaps through the use of conversion courses, it does not provide an immediate solution to the difficulty of balancing technological issues and business requirements.

Additionally, there can be some resistance to training. Students may fear that the time taken to improve their managerial or technical skills will mean that their previous skills have been undermined through neglect. As a result, they may be bypassed for promotion by other staff who have kept their skills up to date.

While this may be less of a difficulty for IT staff who decide to make a firm break from technology, they will still face the complication of convincing organizations to employ someone with substantial IT skills, but only paper qualifications and minimal experience of real business matters. The situation will not improve until senior managers in the IT industry and general businesses are able to recognise and employ the potential of the new hybrid manager resource.

Summary

In this chapter, we have suggested that a result of adoption of technology can be for the organization to fall into the technology trap. Once the effects of the trap are in position, it may become increasingly difficult to deal with those effects. This is because in many organizations computers are treated simply as technology, rather than as components in an information system. This misunderstanding of the place of technology within a business context means that issues may not be fully understood, and as a result the trap is perpetuated.

The example of open systems suggests that implementation of a potentially major new resource, in this case the ability to store, process and distribute large quantities of data with absolute accuracy, may often be carried out using a technical approach. While it may be effective at providing a working system that addresses the functional issues, there are also a large number of other considerations that may be deferred or even omitted from the development process.

The temptation to address only the technological issues is perhaps the greatest danger of the technology trap. If they are addressed at all, security mechanisms may be provided as an afterthought or as a later component in the overall implementation, rather than included and considered as part of the core of the information system. In the next chapter, we will consider the issues of systems development in more detail.

3 Systems development

- **Basics of systems analysis and design**
- **Building security into systems**
- **Identifying system security requirements**
- **Securing the development process**
- **Problem aspects of small and large systems**
- **Standards for secure systems**
- **Involving users in systems development**
- **Summary**

The complexity of modern computer-based information systems is such that, for all but the simplest of examples, they cannot be produced without a considerable amount of planning and preparation beforehand. The actual difficulties of trying to design, develop and implement complex computer-based systems have been recognised since the early 1970s.

In an attempt to deal with what was referred to as the 'Software Crisis', a number of so-called 'methodologies' were advocated. These were a collection of guidelines or ways of working such that computer systems, and in particular software systems, should be designed and developed with a greater degree of success. By using a clear set of rules, or at least reasonably detailed principles, it was possible to ensure that the various tasks of design and development were performed in a methodical, organised fashion, and that no key considerations were omitted, in the opinion of those designing the methodology.

A number of distinct systems development methodologies have been constructed, and some of them are even recognised as 'standards' in their own right. A comparatively successful approach is to identify a number of carefully considered guidelines or techniques that, when applied in a consistent manner, encourage development teams to work in a methodical fashion but still allow them a degree of flexibility in the way that they work.

Regardless of the methodology or set of guidelines that is adopted, the goal is to try to ensure that all relevant details about the desired information system are taken into account during the long and often drawn-out design and development process. Unfortunately, many of the methodologies and guidelines themselves date from the early 1970s and, as a consequence, may not be so well suited for some of today's requirements and constraints.

In this chapter, we will review the major aspects of systems development work, before looking at their implications for the security of modern computer-based information systems.

Basics of systems analysis and design

The material in a textbook or the syllabus for a course on Systems Analysis and Design (SAD) is not intended to be taken as a hard and fast set of rules that must be applied whenever a system is being studied and developed. Quite apart from anything else, the use of SAD techniques does not guarantee that the system will be particularly efficient or effective at the desired tasks, or even that it will work.

There are several clear stages of activity in SAD. The actual number of stages and the tasks performed will vary according to which authority or methodology is being followed. However, in general terms, the sequence of stages would be as follows.

Stage 1: Analysis of the problem

Here, those concerned with developing the new system will go out into the end-user environment and identify key functions that the new system is expected to have. This information will be supplemented by staff preferences and requirements, and any constraints that may be present within the environment such as space, cost and legislation.

After initial analysis has been completed, the key elements of the problem are isolated and verified with the managers and users within the organization, to ensure that the problem *and its context* are understood as fully as possible. Any discrepancies or misunderstandings are fed back into the analysis, and new conclusions presented again. This process will continue until both the systems analysts and the customers are satisfied that all the problems are understood.

Stage 2: Design of the solution

Once the facets of the problem are appreciated, work begins on identifying possible mechanisms for solving them. While it is often recognised that this process must take into account user and staff considerations, in practice the main thrust of effort will often be directed towards the design of a computer-based solution.

A variety of designs may be produced, which are then evaluated according to their predicted level of compliance in solving the problems, and the cost or difficulty of implementing the system.

Stage 3: Implementation of the solution

Having chosen the best design, work begins on implementation. The hardware resources are collected together and configured, and software construction begins. Depending on the approach used to write the software, it may be possible to see a highly simplistic version of the software quickly, or more detailed sub-sections of the overall system as they are produced. The end result is a functional system that should address all the problems identified in stage one.

Stage 4: Testing of the system

From the earliest point at which the need for a new system was recognised, certain criteria were established that the new system should meet. These criteria should be tested to ensure that the system supports the desired functions and provides performance to an acceptable level. This will almost certainly require that the system is tested under conditions which are as near to real-life situations as possible.

For example, real information consisting of known input data and expected output results could be processed by the new system to ensure that the end results are consistent with what should be obtained. Similarly, if a system is expected to provided a minimum level of performance under a heavy workload, then the system should be subjected to *at least* that same workload to ensure that it can cope.

Stage 5: Maintenance of the system

After acceptance by the customer, there may still be some minor or even major changes to be implemented or errors to be corrected. In general, however, acceptance will mean that the customer considers the current performance of the system to be adequate. It may be necessary to modify the system at a later date, perhaps to enhance the performance or to add new functions, or alternatively to revise the implementation, perhaps to reflect changes in procedure, for example following changes in taxation law.

In practice, this final stage of maintenance is one that never finishes, as it will be relevant throughout the whole of the system's functional lifetime.

The benefits and limitations of SAD

The consistent and thoughtful use of SAD techniques should *improve* the chances that the final, delivered system will be produced on time, within budget, and supply the desired set of functions to the customer's satisfaction. Encouraging a great deal more preparation and planning before launching into the actual implementation process is thought to be a 'better' way to develop a system. The hope is that the use of SAD techniques will result in a system that works, and is more effective, if not efficient, at dealing with the specific problems. This should be true regardless of whether the system is automatic, manual, or a combination of the two.

Almost all SAD methodologies are based on the basic five stage model, with various tasks and responsibilities allocated to specific phases in the development process. Throughout, management representatives should be kept advised of what is going on, and how the work is progressing. However, at all times the perspective taken is to focus on the development of a system that will deal with the identified problem. The approach usually adopted is to try to solve the identified problems from a functional perspective that will ultimately achieve the goals needed to improve the operational characteristics of the organization.

This means that only a comparatively small constituent of SAD deals with the actual programming of a computer. Most of the material generated during SAD work will deal with the tasks of analyzing the problems that the computer system must address, identifying the main activities and functions that the computer systems must provide in order to address the identified problems, and working out how each of these derived functions can be constructed such that they will interact and contribute correctly to the problem-solving activity.

Towards the end of the SAD work, there may also be some consideration of how the final systems may be introduced into the working environment. This will tend to emphasise the *way* in which new systems are introduced into the environment. A variety of methods may be used to make the introduction process less painful.

One option is by providing training for novices which, astonishingly, is not always envisaged. Another approach is to use a step-by-step introduction process, where individual groups within the organization are supplied with the system. This is in contrast to a wide-ranging or global introduction where everyone in the organization must use the new system rather than the old system.

Once the system design has been accepted by the customer, it is in a 'finalised form', and from that point on, any modifications cannot easily be 'inserted' into the original system. If changes *are* required, a considerable amount of work might be needed to ensure that the necessary modifications not only comply with the revised analysis of the problem, but also that the design of the changes will be compatible with the earlier design work for the system and, furthermore, that implementation of the changes will not come into conflict with the original implementation details. Therefore, the more planning that is carried out and completed in the earlier stages, so that subsequent changes are not required, the better the chance that the final system will be acceptable to the customer and not be subjected to major - or even minor - modification after delivery.

In reality, however, it is almost inevitable that changes will be required throughout the development process and even after delivery. Recognising this possibility, it can be very tempting for the system developers to allow for subsequent 'bolt-on techno-extensions'. In other words, rather than reapplying the SAD principles to organise the work of inserting newly designed material cleanly into the heart of the original system, independent extensions may be added to the system, possibly making use of 'hooks' within the original system that may have been provided specifically for this purpose. Such an approach is contrary to the philosophy of SAD, but in practice may be considered to be the only commercially viable method of delivering the necessary changes to a system within timescale and budget.

System developers may also be tempted to neglect some of the more administrative aspects of SAD. If a simple modification to a system is required, it can be very frustrating to repeat major stages of the analysis and design process to ensure that the modification is properly designed and will not conflict with the earlier material. Accordingly, a 'quick fix' may be used which will, perhaps, be included in the documentation.

Examples where this is understandable would include changes to screen messages or colors. But evasion of SAD principles is less justifiable for changes in calculations algorithms, or the logic of computerised decisions. Even more difficult is trying to identify the border between what can be permitted and what cannot.

Time and financial incentives may also have drastic effects upon the rigor with which SAD principles are applied. Many developers will have to apply 'quick-and-dirty' fixes in order to supply a functional system. The only hope is that they will have time to document the fix at a later date, although commercial pressures and deadlines accumulate to make this less and less likely.

We therefore conclude that even the 'better' approach of using formal methodologies cannot guarantee that the development process will be smooth and trouble-free, or even that the methodologies will be applied rigorously throughout.

Building security into systems

We now turn to the specific objective of developing *secure* computer-based information systems. There are two main approaches that may be taken to achieve this.

The first is to deal with security mechanisms very early on in the development process. This has the advantage that the protection mechanisms can be designed and subsequently implemented at the very heart of the system. As a result, they have direct and much greater influence over any applications that are used on the system. Therefore, the level of protection that can be provided on the system is much greater. The disadvantage of this approach is that it is only possible to provide such deep-rooted security mechanisms if a complete new system is being developed from the very beginning.

A second approach may be used for reasons of reduced cost and effort, or because extreme security is not required, or simply because the first approach cannot be utilized. Here, security mechanisms are applied to an existing system in a manner that *supplements* the conventional system features.

This method has the advantage that its implementation can be much quicker and easier than building a complete system 'from scratch' and, furthermore, may allow the customer organization more choice as to which systems will be employed in the first place.

The disadvantage is that the protection mechanisms are not so deeply embedded, which means that applications running on the system may, in theory, be able to bypass the security devices. This must undermine the overall security of the system.

Security kernels

The philosophy of the first approach is often referred to by using the term 'security kernel'. This means that the goal of building security into a system is achieved by providing an extremely secure core or 'kernel' for the entire system. This kernel has direct control over the major resources of the computer. No other functions at any other level can occur without being performed, and implicitly 'approved', by the security kernel. A variety of models are possible for implementing security kernels, and they generally derive from work done on the development of military information systems.

Military systems describe data items or 'objects' as having one of several basic levels of security categorisation. In order of increasing sensitivity, these are: Unclassified, Restricted, Confidential, Secret and Top Secret. Other levels may also be defined according to need, for example Unclassified But Sensitive for material between Unclassified and Restricted. It should be noted that the more levels there are, the more difficult it can become to agree on the difference between them.

Objects may only be accessed, or read, by users or 'subjects' that have the appropriate level of authority or 'clearance' for that particular task. Thus a user with permission to access material up to Secret level could read data in the

Unclassified, Confidential and Secret levels. Permission of this kind is often called *read-down*. The same user would not be allowed access to Top Secret documents.

Interestingly, users can always produce data to a higher classification than they are themselves. Thus a user who has clearance to Secret levels could write a document that is subsequently classified as Top Secret.

The opposite is not always true. In theory, a user with Secret clearance is capable of writing a general purpose document that would be described as Confidential or even Unclassified. This is because the user is able to identify the sensitive material and omit any references to it. However, when dealing with computer-based information systems, a user of the system may not always be a human being; this is why the term 'subject' is generally preferred to 'user'. The subject in a computer system *could* be a human user, but could also be a program acting on behalf of a user, or even a program not acting directly on behalf of a human user, such as a program that automatically performs a regular backup of data.

We therefore have the situation where the subject might be non-human, and would not be able to identify which components of Secret material should be omitted in order for the new material to be described as Confidential or Unclassified. Accordingly, the subject cannot be allowed to create objects at a lower security classification.

Security kernels are widely regarded as the mechanism which enables the highest possible level of confidence in the security of computer systems. However, by definition, they can only be implemented at the very heart of new systems. Insertion of a security kernel into an existing system would require such a major redesign and reimplementation that it could not be considered as a cost-effective process.

This means that security kernels are only suitable for those organizations that can or must develop a complete system from the very beginning, using only the most elementary components or working to a precise 'custom-built' specification. Consequently, security kernels will be of less use for the majority of organizations that may prefer to append security mechanisms onto existing or 'off-the-shelf' systems.

The alternative to security kernels

The only practical alternative for most organizations will be to develop their own systems using existing applications as far as possible. In most cases these systems will be constructed to work on 'standard' hardware configurations, and certainly using a 'standard' operating system. This means that it will be almost impossible to implement a security kernel at the heart of the organization's new system, as the kernel would then be dependent upon hardware and operating system components that may not be secure themselves.

The reality is that for the majority of organizational computer-based information systems, security will be seen as an issue that can be considered throughout the development process, but which is actually dealt with as an independent activity, distinct from the development of the central system. This is not to say that security is ignored, but often the view is taken that the tasks of providing security mechanisms can be addressed as a separate issue.

Consequently, security issues may be deferred until the system is in the latter stages of development, or until it is finally 'up-and-running'. Even then, security will only be addressed if it is still thought to be necessary. Perhaps the only aspect of security, in its broadest sense, that *will* be actively addressed throughout the development work is for the provision of mechanisms that deal with threats arising from *accidental* systems software or hardware failure.

In most cases, this means that arrangements are made for the system to support backups or fault tolerance mechanisms. The urgency with which these issues are addressed will reflect previous experiences of hardware, support software, and similar systems in other organizations. Priority is only given to system support measures if someone within the organization has reason to believe that there is, or might be, a problem with the proposed system.

However, it may save resources and also improve the overall security of the system if such issues could be addressed and incorporated into the design activities at an early stage. Just as essential is the importance of making the development process secure itself. This is necessary to ensure that any new system cannot be altered, modified or extended at some point during the development or following delivery, without all aspects of the changes being very carefully monitored, considered, planned and controlled; indeed as *part* of the original SAD work. The difficulty is that such a requirement may not be practical where cost-effectiveness will be a high priority consideration, especially given that many organizations will not expect to suffer from security threats to their new system. For most SAD methods, it is not possible to provide sufficient cost-justification for this level of development administration overhead.

Identifying system security requirements

A very helpful source of advice and guidance for this task would be the members of an auditing team. As well as being concerned with the facts and figures of the company accounts, and approving budget details, auditors will be keen to ensure that accurate and thorough information is available to them. As part of this task, audit teams will be very interested in security. Security of the organization, as well as protection measures for backups and software controls can all be considered as part of the audit process. Attention will be paid to operating system software as well as application software, because no amount of security provided within an application program will help secure the system if the underlying environment has weaknesses or loopholes that might be exploited.

In many cases, auditors are concerned with minimising the chance of errors, but their efforts may have the beneficial side-effect of reducing the opportunity for deliberate fraud. Getting involved during the initial work on analysis and design of the system enables auditors to act as consultants and security experts, making suggestions and recommendations on what forms of controls and security mechanisms will be required, where they should be located within the system, and the effects that such controls and mechanisms will have on the system as a whole.

These considerations are particularly important when the processing and distribution of data by a computer system can extend beyond a company's borders, perhaps using applications that share information such as Electronic Data Interchange (EDI) or Electronic Fund Transfer at Point of Sale (EFT/POS) packages. Organizations cannot take the narrow perspective of considering only their own systems. They must also recognise the other external systems with which they will exchange data. The capacity for sharing data means that the organization will be expected to protect other organization's data and organizational interests as well.

This consideration may become even more important following any adoption of the concept of *keiretsu*, or business groups, as defined and utilized by many Japanese organizations and managers. Here, a close-knit community of interdependent businesses cooperate to achieve a variety of mutually acceptable objectives.

Security features must ensure that it is impossible to access actual working data without authorization. In addition, it is important that the *components* of the system cannot themselves be accessed. This is because anyone who can obtain a copy of the original programs used to build the systems, may be able to implement a modified version, perhaps to work as a trojan horse. Given the right opportunity, the trojan horse could then be inserted into the system ready to wreak havoc. It is not sufficient to protect just data and other information on the system. It is also vital to protect the software itself, as it is of primary importance for the processing of the data, not to mention its value in terms of time and money invested.

A major part of the access control mechanisms will inevitably be based upon passwords. However, the security of passwords can be undermined. One of the greatest threats arises from a natural human tendency to choose words or

Table 2: Distribution of actual passwords in 1979 survey

Number of instances	Percentage of total	Type of password
15	0.5%	A single ASCII character
72	2%	Two ASCII characters
464	14%	Three ASCII characters
477	14.5%	Four alphabetic characters
706	21.5%	Five alphabetic characters
605	18.5%	Six lower case alphabetic characters
492	15%	Words in dictionary or list of names
458	14%	Other

phrases that are easy to remember - and hence guess. A survey was carried out by Robert Morris and Ken Thompson and reported in the Communications of the ACM, November 1979 (see table 2). 3,289 passwords were gathered from users and analyzed. This showed that around 71% of the passwords used only six letters or less.

If such a system was subjected to a brute force attack, for example the kind carried out by the Internet Worm described in chapter one, all possible passwords based on up to six alphabetical characters could be checked in about 89 hours, assuming one check every 1 millisecond. In practice, the checks would not take this long, and a variety of common passwords could be tried first in order to cut down the search time.

Even if a sensible password is chosen, the user may be tempted not to change it unless forced to. Even if there is no reason to suspect that the security of a password has been compromised, it makes sense to change to a new password frequently in order to reduce the effectiveness of a brute force approach, or in case someone gets hold of an old password list.

Some users may be tempted to try and record the current password by writing it down somewhere. This is particularly true if the password is computer-generated, or it is not particularly memorable, for example 'aedtgyj'. Documenting a password like this makes security impossible.

Passwords may seem to be rather an 'old' technology. However, *if* sensible generation and protection techniques are used, and *if* passwords are used properly, then they represent an extremely cost-effective way of providing substantial levels of security. It is essential to emphasise the need for sensible password management. This is because, in a sense, passwords represent an *insecurity* measure, because they allow access to an otherwise secure system.

The Trusted Computing Base

In addition to establishing specific mechanisms for implementing security, it is also important to identify logical sections or compartments of the system that are to be kept distinct from the remainder of the system, and which can be better protected from compromise. These sections, often referred to as the 'Trusted Computing Base,' or TCB, provide a base from which the remainder of the system can function with the corresponding degree of security. In practice, a TCB may be a security kernel, or it may be an entire trusted computer system. In order to implement a TCB, six fundamental requirements must be met, many of which can be applied to the development of other mechanisms.

Security policy An explicit and well-defined policy must exist which is enforced by the system. This enables the system to determine if access to an object is granted to a subject.

Marking Access control labels must be associated with objects. These identify the object's sensitivity level, and the various modes of access available to subjects that may access the object.

Identification Access is controlled according to the subject that seeks access and the object classifications that they are authorized to access.

Accountability Audit information is required so that activities can be traced to the subject responsible.

Assurance The computer system provides mechanisms that guarantee the Policy, Marking, Identification and Accountability requirements. These mechanisms will be implemented deep within the system, and it will be possible to examine independently the sufficiency of each.

Continuous protection The mechanisms which provide the basic requirements are themselves continuously protected against unauthorized changes or tampering.

In implementing these requirements, three system features will be necessary:

Mandatory security controls These provide access controls so that authorized users may perform tasks, while unauthorized users will not gain access. Classified data cannot be moved freely within the system, and in particular data cannot be moved to a storage area of lower classification without appropriate revisions being performed and approval obtained. The users will have no choice but to comply with these controls.

Discretionary security controls These are less strict controls which enable the user to provide additional restriction to existing controls. They supplement rather than replace mandatory access controls.

Labelling controls As already described, these enable the mandatory and discretionary controls to function by ensuring that all items can be labelled with security and privacy classification information. The labels are inseparable from the items to which they refer. They allow the controls to be properly and consistently enforced.

Securing the development process

In one sense, the responsibility for securing the development process is simple: everyone at all levels within the organization has a direct duty to comply with and promote general security matters, not just those issues relating to computer security. We will return to this theme in a later chapter with regard to the difficulty of spreading the message of security. However, in our present discussion, we are interested in the technological security of computer systems during development.

An active approach to the development and management of system security should be taken, and this should be present throughout all system development tasks. This can be achieved through the adoption of proven control techniques, and by promoting good practices within the system and beyond its boundaries into the organization. In this way, these controls are more likely to become corporate standards.

Throughout the systems development process, regular checks should be made to look for any programs or 'modules' that attempt to modify data where this is unexpected. In particular, checks should focus upon regular examination of major components of data, such as dates, names and account numbers. Additionally, a regular check should be made to ensure that the functions performed by the system are the only ones which it should be performing.

It is important to keep a constant watch during the development process, checking for any sign of security breaches. This is performed by regularly examining programs and system libraries for unknown or unexpected components, checking for new implementations or new procedures, and at all times fully documenting all decisions, changes and modifications in order to ensure consistency and authorization for the changes. By performing regular and thorough checks, the opportunities for violation of the system during develop-ment will be reduced and, in the event that an error is detected, it should be at a sufficiently early stage that no significant damage will have been caused and there will still be time for corrections to be made.

In reality, very few organizations are able or, in some cases, even willing, to carry out this kind of rigorous checking procedure. The most understandable reason for this is the perceived lack of resources available. Even with the maximum possible allocation of staff to the development work, there is little chance of the final system being delivered on time and to full specification. Therefore, it is difficult to justify the appointment of staff to a monitoring function that will not contribute directly to the development process, and may actively serve to delay the work carried out.

With the exception of those organizations which have computer system development as a major business function, it is rare to encounter any form of quality assurance functions in most computer departments of organizations. The nearest equivalent will be some of the work performed by auditors. Of necessity however, this cannot be the full-time and in-detail monitoring that might be ideal.

For system development to be performed with sufficient attention to security, it is very important to determine the domain within the organization which should have responsibility for the security of the development of a computer-based information system. Without this identification, consideration of security will not be encouraged and promoted and, as a result, important aspects may be neglected or overlooked.

It may appear that the responsibility should be automatically assigned to the Information Technology Services Department, or some equivalent. Certainly much of the work can be carried out by IT services. However, the emphasis of these departments will naturally tend to be upon maintaining the technological aspects of computer security. Consequently, it is possible for other, non-technological, aspects to be neglected.

An alternative approach that may be used increasingly in the future is to recruit the power of the computer systems themselves. Already, computers are important for designing and developing computer electronics and the other hardware components. To some extent, the systems can contribute to the development of software using dedicated automatic tools. This process is usually referred to as Computer Aided Software Engineering or CASE, although it can relate to the complete set of software, hardware and environmental considerations.

CASE tools are intended to assist human developers with the tasks that are carried out during system construction. In particular, they address issues of consistency in design and implementation, and also deal with many of the less interesting chores such as documenting the system and any changes, and monitoring progress.

There is no reason why automation of the development process should not be extended to address security issues as well. Naturally, an automated security tool of this kind would have to perform stringent integrity checks on itself, to ensure that its own functions and activities were not being compromised in some way. However, given a standardized environment, it should be possible to provide the development team with a 'black box' tool that would perform many of the supervisory tasks that security objectives would require.

It must be realised however that such tools would not guarantee that the developed system is completely secure. Also, the tools could only provide a degree of assurance that the development process was secure, and that the resulting system did not deviate from design and functional specifications, except where agreed as part of a revised specification. Any errors in the design, or subsequent fixes or enhancements could still create accidental or deliberate side-effects, and these might not be detected by the automated tools in a CASE environment owing to limitations in the original CASE system specification. A CASE tool cannot detect errors for which it is not configured.

Problem aspects of small and large systems

Once a computer-based information system is installed, it can be very difficult to make significant changes to the internal nature of the system. Accordingly, there are situations where security measures cannot be applied with the complete flexibility needed in order to optimise the protection.

The most obvious example of this derives from the architecture of the desk-top personal computer. A PC is not necessarily an information system, but it may used as part of one. This is where many difficulties can arise.

When the PC was first planned by IBM, it was not expected to be a particularly successful system. Projected sales were estimated in thousands rather than millions. Therefore, much of the attention to detail emphasised cost-effectiveness and straightforward price performance characteristics. Most notable was the complete absence of any meaningful forms of computer security mechanisms.

As the PC became more and more widely used, so the demand grew for more and more performance from the system. Larger quantities of memory, faster processing speeds, and better displays were all expected by consumers who recognised the potential of the small computer. Many of the demands were fulfilled by third party organizations making use of the intrinsic expandability of the PC and offering plug-in cards that provided extra facilities.

However, in designing the improvements to the basic system, it was, and remains, essential to maintain compatibility with the 'standard' configuration. Otherwise, the end result is an improved but possibly unstable system, resulting from incompatibilities.

The absence of any significant security mechanisms in the standard PC architecture has been overcome by some firms using hardware or software combinations. However, the systems must inevitably make the protected PC distinctly different from the standard, and this has resulted in some difficulties for organizations that take this approach.

An alternative method of securing the hardware is for the organization to have a clear overall policy with regard to PC and other small-scale computer technology. The idea behind this approach is to recognise that some systems cannot be made secure, but it may be possible to locate them in a secure environment. This requires that guidelines or policies are developed which specify how otherwise insecure systems, such as PCs, are to be acquired and allocated within an organization. However, the cheapness and portability of PCs means that they can bypass normal administrative procedures, often appearing at short notice as a result of easily approved petty cash requests. They can also relocate very easily within the organization - or even worse, outside the organization.

A well-publicised example of this sort of threat occurred just prior to the Gulf War, when a laptop PC was among documents and other items stolen on December 17 1990 from the car of RAF Wing Commander David Farquhar. It happened as he was returning to RAF Strike Command following a briefing with the British Prime Minister at Downing Street. Although never confirmed, the extensive measures taken at the time to suppress news of the loss suggested to many commentators that the PC held classified material relevant to planned Gulf strategies.

On larger computer systems such as mini-computers or mainframes, security measures may be provided as optional extras for the underlying operating system. Some security mechanisms will be built into the standard system as supplied, but there are documented cases where these facilities prove less than adequate. One manufacturer that has suffered problems is Digital Equipment Corporation (DEC) with its VMS operating system software for use on the VAX range of computers. DEC has always been particularly strong with respect to networking its computers, and this has made them a popular target for hackers. Early VMS systems did not have a security manual, and the software itself came with weak file protection and default passwords that people very rarely changed.

Today, the security of VMS has been greatly improved, not least by building a Distributed Systems Security Architecture (DSSA) into new releases. DSSA provides far more security features than were available in the earlier versions of VMS.

The difficulty for manufacturers is that large systems will necessarily support many more users doing a variety of different tasks. It is essential that users, their data and their tasks can be prevented from interfering or interacting with each other.

It may not be possible for a manufacturer to take full advantage of new ideas and technology as they are developed. Unlike small computers, the hardware base of mini-computers and mainframe computers will often be derived from somewhat dated architectures in order to maintain compatibility with existing systems. This is necessary in view of the substantial investment by users and manufacturers in the technology.

Complicating the matter is the observation that the computing capability of many small machines can now actually equal or exceed that of a large system. Furthermore, a large system may 'evolve' from the interconnection of many smaller machines. Such networks may be implemented using a variety of technologies, but in any case they implicitly cause verification problems since the systems must establish whether a user is who he says he is, and whether he is authorized to perform the task that is requested. In a networked system, where multiple computers may share workloads or resources - and in the most advanced configurations operate in a transparently distributed fashion - many users do not like having to reconfirm identity having once established it in order to gain initial access.

There is also a distinction in the security mechanisms required. The difference between them is measured in terms of 'securable systems' and 'secure instances' of the systems. A securable system is one that can be secured in its own right, perhaps by inclusion of a security kernel. A secure instance of a system is where the system, not necessarily secure in its own right, is placed into a controlled environment.

Quite clearly, smaller computers such as personal computers and the larger workstations can function, and are often installed, in everyday offices and workplaces. The small computers are not securable systems, and are normally used in insecure instances.

By contrast, the larger machines such as mainframes and minicomputers are often located in dedicated computer rooms. This means that, from the physical perspective, the larger computers are usually in an environment that can be controlled more easily. From the system perspective, larger computers are normally multi-user and multi-tasking, and so greater effort goes into the implementation and support for distinct operational domains within the system.

The capacity of small systems used to be such that only minimal amounts of data could be retained, and the overall reliability of the system was such that they were never used as the sole storage and processing facility. More recently, the smaller machines have gained considerably in terms of speed and capacity, but the way in which these machines are viewed has not changed in parallel. They are still viewed as simple, cheap desk-top machines.

Thus, larger computers are securable systems to a much greater degree than smaller systems. However, it is possible to envisage instances where the specific installation results in a contrary situation. Smaller computers can be made almost impregnable, although this would mean that a special effort must be made to try and implement the necessary mechanisms. Equally, larger computers can very easily be made non-secure, although a considerable degree of incompetence must be tolerated for this to happen. In practice, such a degree of laxity would probably manifest itself in many other ways that would be revealed during system administration procedures.

Standards for secure systems

In order to improve upon the process of systems development, it may be possible to standardize some aspects. This may be of benefit to organizations in a number of ways. In theory, if a system is constructed using components which all meet certain standards, then the resulting system should also meet, or come close to meeting, the same standards. Alternatively, by using security standards as a model for the design of customised systems, it is possible that the development process can be directed towards providing the desired level of protection.

Not surprisingly, details of some computer security standards are not widely publicised; however, the most notable exception concerns the US Department of Defense 'Trusted Computer System Evaluation Criteria' or TCSEC. A more recent European equivalent is the 'Information Technology Security Evaluation Criteria' or ITSEC. Both of these represent standard measures against which products can be compared. An organization wishing to have its software or hardware product evaluated makes use of an accredited evaluation authority, which carries out the full and formal evaluation process.

The Trusted Computer System Evaluation Criteria

This US Department of Defense (DoD) standard is described in a volume which is often referred to by the title 'Orange Book', owing to the color of its cover. The first publication was in 1983, with a substantially revised edition issued in 1985. The intention of the criteria was to fulfil three purposes:

- 'To provide a standard for manufacturers as to what security features to build into their new and planned, commercial products in order to provide widely available systems that satisfy trust requirements (with particular emphasis on preventing the disclosure of data) for sensitive applications'.
- 'To provide DoD components with a metric with which to evaluate the degree of trust that can be placed in computer systems for the secure processing of classified and other information'.
- 'To provide a basis for specifying security requirements in acquisition specifications'.

The TCSEC describes a Trusted Computing Base using four divisions, A, B, C and D. Most of the divisions are subdivided into classes, as shown in table 3. Division A, which only has a single class A1, represents the most secure TCB; while Division D, which again has the single class D, is the least secure TCB.

The process of evaluating a software or hardware product for certification to one of the levels described above is only open to US products. However, the wide acceptance of the TCSEC means that overseas products are sometimes described, for example, as 'offering C2 level security'.

The Information Technology Security Evaluation Criteria

Although well-known outside the US, the TCSEC are not formally recognised elsewhere. The fact that the TCSEC was produced specifically for US purposes has encouraged other countries to produce their own standards, not least so that non-US manufacturers can submit their products for evaluation and certification.

In the United Kingdom, the Department of Trade and Industry (DTI) and the Government Communications Headquarters (GCHQ) produced a series of 'Green Books' for the Commercial Computer Security Centre (CCSC).

Other European nations have also been active in this area. In Germany, the German Information Security Agency (GISA) produced a 'Criteria for the Evaluation of the Trustworthiness of Information Technology (IT) Systems' (ZSIEC), and the French Service Central de la Sécurité des Systèmes d'Information (SCSSI) issued a Catalogue de Critères Destinés à évaluer le Degré de Confiance des Systèmes d'Information.

Table 3: The Trusted Computer System Evaluation Criteria categories

Class	Sub-class	Meaning
A Verified Protection	A1 Verified Design	Formal design specification and verification analysis to ensure correct implementation of TCB.
B Mandatory Protection	B3 Security Domains	Tamperproof monitoring of all object accesses by subjects. Exclusion of code not essential to security enforcement. System engineered for minimum complexity. Full audit of security-relevant events.
	B2 Structured Protection	Formal security policy applying discretionary and mandatory access control to all subjects and objects.
	B1 Labelled Security Protection	Informal security policy. Data labelling and mandatory access control over named objects. Exported information must be accurately labelled.
C Discretionary Protection	C2 Controlled Access Protection	Substantial discretionary access controls. Users are accountable for actions through login procedures, auditing of security-relevant events, and resource isolation.
	C1 Discretionary Security Protection	Nominal discretionary access controls. Access limitations can be enforced. In practice, represents an environment where users cooperate in processing data at the same levels of sensitivity.
D Minimal Protection	D Minimal Protection	All systems that fail to meet higher evaluation criteria.

Given the range of standards with comparable aims, and in order to reflect the imminent creation of a unified Europe, a decision was taken by four European nations - France, Germany, the Netherlands and the United Kingdom - to harmonise their work on information security standards, with a view to developing a single standard combining the best features from each of the national initiatives. The result was that on 2 May 1990, the first draft of the Information Technology Security Evaluation Criteria (ITSEC) was issued. The white cover immediately led to the text being referred to as the 'White Book'.

Comments on the draft were invited, and in June 1991 a revised document was issued describing the provisional harmonised criteria. This was adopted for use within the European Community for a two-year period to allow practical experience to be used to further review and develop the standard.

Table 4: Predefined functionality classes, from draft ITSEC

1990 ITSEC	1991 ITSEC	Interpretation
F10	F-DX	Intended for networks with high demands on the confidentiality and integrity of the information to be communicated
F9	F-DC	Intended for TOEs with high demands for confidentiality of data during data communications
F8	F-DI	Identifies high requirements for safeguarding data integrity during data communications
F7	F-AV	Identifies requirements for the availability of a complete TOE or special functions
F6	F-IN	Identifies high integrity requirements for data and programs
F5	F-B3	Provides functions to support distinct security administration duties, and auditing of security relevant events. Derived from TCSEC classes B3 and A1
F4	F-B2	Mandatory access controls extended to all subjects and objects. Authentication requirements of F-B1 are strengthened. Derived from TCSEC class B2
F3	F-B1	Sensitivity labels are supported, and used to enforce a set of mandatory access controls over subjects and objects. Derived from TCSEC class B1
F2	F-C2	Greater precision in discretionary access control. Users are accountable for actions using identification procedures, auditing of security relevant events, and resource isolation. Derived from TCSEC class C2
F1	F-C1	Discretionary access control. Derived from TCSEC class C1
F0	No equivalent	Minimal protection

The ITSEC are applied to a Target of Evaluation (TOE), which is the product or system being assessed. The TCB in a TOE is defined as consisting of system components which directly contribute to satisfying security objectives - and hence are security enforcing; and other components that are not security enforcing but which must be present and operating correctly for security to be enforced - these are security relevant.

The functionality of the TOE consists of all the security functions taken as a whole. The functionality will be considered from three perspectives.

Table 5: The ITSEC classes of confidence

Evaluation level	Summary
E6	As E5, with formal specification of security enforcing functions and architectural design
E5	As E4, with close correspondence between detailed design and source code
E4	As E3, with underlying formal model of security policy. Security enforcing functions, architectural design and detailed design specified in a semi-formal style
E3	As E2, with source code and hardware corresponding to security mechanisms. Evidence of testing of the mechanisms is also required
E2	As E1, with informal description of detailed design. Evidence of functional testing, a configuration control system and approved distribution procedures are required
E1	A security target for the TOE is defined, and an informal description of the architectural design of the TOE provided. Functional testing is performed to show that the TOE meets its security target
E0	Level of inadequate assurance

- Security objectives - why the functionality is wanted.
- Security functions - what functionality is actually provided.
- Security mechanisms - how the functionality is provided.

Many systems will have a number of similar objectives in providing security. Accordingly, there are a number of common sets of security functions that can be identified. The ITSEC in its current draft form describes ten examples, listed in table 4. It is possible for a TOE to be assigned to several functionality classes at the same time. In keeping with their correspondence to the TCSEC classes, F-C1, F-C2, F-B1, F-B2 and F-B3 are hierarchically ordered. However, the remainder of the classes may be combined.

After identifying its functionality, the TOE can then be assessed for confidence in effectiveness and correctness. The effectiveness of the TOE is assessed by whether the functionality of the TOE will satisfy the stated security objectives. This involves considering the suitability of the functions, how well they work together, the consequences of known or discovered vulnerabilities, and overall ease of use.

The correctness of the TOE concerns the implementation of the security functions. As shown in table 5, seven evaluation labels are defined, from E0 to

Table 6: Comparison between TCSEC and ITSEC classes

1991 ITSEC	US TCSEC	Interpretation
F-B3, E6	A1	Verified design
F-B3, E5	B3	Security domains
F-B2, E4	B2	Structured protection
F-B1, E3	B1	Labelled security protection
F-C2, E2	C2	Controlled access protection
F-C1, E1	C1	Discretionary protection
E0	D	Minimal protection

E6. Each of these represents clearly defined and increasing levels of confidence that the TOE has been correctly constructed; and furthermore that the construction was performed using a demonstrably correct development process and development environment. E0 represents inadequate confidence in the correctness. E1 represents an entry point of no useful confidence, while E6 represents the highest level of confidence.

It is interesting to compare the combined functionality and confidence ITSEC classes with their corresponding classes in the TCSEC, as shown in table 6. It should be noted that in some classes, the correspondence is not absolute.

As with the TCSEC, the ITSEC are not necessarily of direct use to organizations that simply require to develop their own computer-based information system. The purpose of both sets of criteria is to provide a scale by which the security of hardware or software products may be assessed. However, in doing so, the criteria identify goals that may be used by organizations to identify the levels of security that their system will require, and the corresponding functional characteristics.

For example, an organization implementing a system with a very high level of security might be aiming for ITSEC level E3, or TCSEC level B1, or above. An examination of the standards indicates the features of systems which meet such levels, emphasising the importance of labelling of objects and mandatory access control over named objects.

The source code of the system and the hardware must demonstrably correspond to the desired security mechanisms. For many businesses, these requirements may be in excess of what is required. For other organizations, such as banks which normally process very high value material, these levels of security would be essential.

Identification of mechanisms and the way in which they contribute to the overall security of the system is an important part of the system development process. Implementation of some mechanisms may be deferred to later stages, while others, such as labelling of objects, must necessarily be addressed in earlier stages.

Involving users in system development

Basic system functions can normally be identified with comparative ease *before* a computer system is put in place. However, before long, it becomes much more difficult to accommodate further changes to the system, as these may significantly alter the way in which a user identifies and selects 'necessary' functions.

At the same time, trying to make provision for all eventualities not only increases the demands made upon the developers, but also introduces a further set of problems. As more advanced functions and facilities are provided by the system, users naturally start to take advantage of them. This can have advantages and disadvantages.

There are many facilities provided by computer systems that users would be reluctant to relinquish once they have been adopted. Word-processor users might be loath to return to typewriters or long-hand notes. Spreadsheet users are able to build complex models that perform detailed calculation in seconds, where the manual equivalent would be almost impossible. Electronic mail users may view the computer-assisted processing of information sharing as demonstrable evidence of the value of technology.

Once a particular facility has been made available in an information system, users will either adopt it or neglect it. The enthusiasm with which a function is utilized reflects the level of contribution that the function makes to the user's job function. If a function or facility is particularly effective, the user will rapidly come to depend upon its continued availability.

If for any reason that function is subsequently taken away, or constrained in some fashion; then the users may experience considerable difficulty in returning to an older style of working.

For similar reasons, users will be unwilling to adopt and utilize 'difficult' systems. These may be defined as systems which are not intuitive to use, or which have irritating or unnecessary operational characteristics. There may be limitations that confine the tasks that can be performed by the system. If users do consider a system to be difficult to use, then they may not even bother to make the effort of trying to use it.

Equally, systems that attempt to do 'everything' may be just as infuriating. A package that offers every conceivable option for performing a particular task may actually be difficult to use. This could be due to the additional time or command complexity required to specify precisely which function is required.

One trend in software development that has failed to do as well as expected has been the so-called 'integrated package'. The goal was to produce a single software system that would provide all the functions that a user could possibly wish for. Furthermore, all of the functions could 'cooperate' with each other, so that the package should be easy to learn and easier to use.

In practice, this approach has been characterised by a distinct lack of success. So far, no single integrated package in any computer environment has ever succeeded in providing all the necessary functions that users want. At best, the package will perform a limited sub-set of the necessary tasks; but once the functional boundary has been crossed, and the limits of the package reached, the productivity of the user cannot be increased further.

Today, the only type of integrated package that could conceivably be described as successful refers to the collection of small utilities or 'applets' provided by Graphic User Interfaces such as Microsoft Windows or OS/2. An applet is a limited tool, such as a card-index style of database, or a text-processor suitable for typing letters rather than books. Each of these applets will have been designed to exchange data with the other applets, wherever possible.

But system development also refers to the environment within which the technology, both hardware and software, will be used. A series of guidelines or policies must be developed that specify non-technical aspects of information system security.

Within this environment, the contribution of users to the development of such security policies can be very wide-ranging. They will be directly involved with the computer systems and will therefore experience the effects of security measures at first hand. These measures will often appear to users in the form of constraints. Alternatively, it may appear that the measures result in slower response times from the system, or perhaps it takes longer for the user to get to a point at which useful work can be done.

Involving users does not mean that they must be told about every security mechanism and how it works, but rather it ensures that users are more likely to appreciate why the mechanisms must be put in place, and to realise that there will inevitably be some effects upon their normal tasks. The goal is to try to obtain their cooperation and compliance in following the policies.

There is an additional advantage to involving users in the development process. They will be of great assistance in identifying particular areas that must be addressed. Since they are directly concerned with the tasks that must be performed, users have a practical understanding of the system, and its weaknesses and strengths.

On the other hand, there are disadvantages to involving users. The most obvious difficulty is that in discussing security issues, any weaknesses may be highlighted to users who would otherwise remain unaware of the threats. However, a decision not to involve users in the security policy development process cannot guarantee that users stay ignorant of weaknesses. At any time, a user may discover a loophole in the system. Accordingly, it may be preferable for the discussion of security issues to take place in a controlled environment, so that the communication of the ideas can take place in an ordered fashion.

Furthermore, if users are involved in identifying any weaknesses in a system, they may take the opportunity to deliberately compromise the system. For example, they may neglect to mention weaknesses in the hope of exploiting them later. Alternatively, the users might pretend to identify the existence of deficiencies in an attempt to influence the new system, or to distract attention away from actual problems. This could be for reasons of maintaining territorial control, or empire-building, or even a form of revenge against the employer. In practice, such claims could be verified and hence disproved fairly easily, and in fact are of benefit in calling into question the loyalty or competence of the original user.

The ideas which are put forward by users can be taken into account during the development of computer security policies. However, the actual gravity with which the ideas are considered may vary according to circumstance. For example, if a number of ideas are proposed by a large sample of users, and there is a high level of similarity between the ideas, then it is more likely that the suggestions are valid.

Conversely, unusual suggestions, or ideas from a very small sample of users, should be treated with more caution. In any case, the ideas should be checked by an independent method to establish validity. Any claimed weakness or deficiency in a system could be observed by careful examination of the system, either by visual inspection or 'behind-the-scenes' task monitoring.

When a selection of security mechanisms have been identified for solving a particular threat, it may be considered a valuable exercise to try them out in a real user environment. However, in an attempt to identify the ideal balance point between ease-of-use and minimum acceptable security, care should be taken to ensure that the evaluation does not produce results biased in favor of ease-of-use.

Provision of functionality in a computer system must take into account the practicalities of user requirements and perspectives. If the user is not satisfied with a system for any reason, its success will be, at best, severely constrained.

Summary

Development of software and systems is an extremely difficult task. Even an application as apparently straightforward as a spreadsheet tool requires many man-years of effort, and the final collection of program code would fill a telephone book. It is not surprising therefore if difficulties occur.

Reputations can be ruined and lives threatened by programming mistakes. Software is used to control aircraft, medical technology and entire financial systems. Yet much of the work will be done by young programmers who work in 18-hour 'blitzes', oblivious to the world outside. Other professions may view software development as a 'cowboy' activity with poor self-discipline. This explains the need to improve software reliability, and a major component of that task is to improve system security, and the management of systems development.

The adoption and implementation of standards, not least in the development process, may be of assistance in improving the correctness of systems, and in subsequently increasing the confidence that users and owners may have in their systems.

4 Management considerations

- **Managers, strategies, and information**
- **The danger of organizational dependencies**
- **Why managers must be involved**
- **Business objectives and computer security**
- **Identifying the options**
- **Management of security**
- **Summary**

Computer security relates not only to the protection of the system and the data being processed, but additionally to the well-being and continued profitability of the organization. Security can no longer be delegated to a single department, or implemented using security guards. Security of technology is a strategic issue and must therefore be addressed by managers.

In this chapter, we look at some of the managerial issues that must be considered for the security of computer-based information systems. The discussion is not intended to provide a manager's checklist for securing computer systems. There are plenty of excellent texts and materials for this purpose. It is more important to examine the issues *in the context of the organization*, and it is this perspective that is of interest here.

Managers, strategies, and information
There are many different definitions of a 'manager'. For our purposes, a suitable working definition of a manager is anyone who is charged with, and is responsible for, the task of administering a variety of resources, for the purpose of benefiting the organization.

The resources may be people, equipment, budgets, or a combination of these. The major tasks of administration will require the manager to identify, plan, implement, monitor and perhaps modify the performance of appropriate actions.

The actions themselves will usually be performed by the staff resources of the organization, which by definition includes all the managers as well. Plans are devised with a view to identifying methods by which objectives may be achieved, and thus reflect the strategies of the organization which are the broad outlines defining how an organization will achieve its objectives.

71

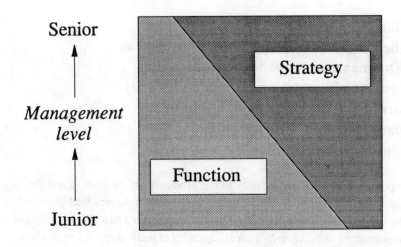

Figure 5: The varying responsibility of managerial levels

The nature of the manager's role will vary according to the position he holds within the organization, as shown in figure 5. A senior manager will be more concerned with the strategy for the organization as a whole. The details of implementation, while important, are of less concern to the senior manager.

By contrast, junior managers receive their instructions from more senior colleagues in the form of strategic goals. They then have the role of administering to tasks which, as a whole, bring about the realisation of the chosen strategies. This means that junior managers will be more interested in the functional nature of the tasks that must be performed.

However, all managers, at all levels, must be aware of strategic and functional issues to some degree. A senior manager cannot produce a strategy without taking into consideration some of the practical aspects of *how* that strategy will be implemented.

Similarly, junior managers are more likely to be effective in their duties if they have some understanding of how and why their efforts contribute to the overall direction of the organization. This enables them to select optimised actions to perform tasks.

The concepts of strategy and function are particularly dependent upon a resource such as information, since the presence or absence of information influences them both. This is because managers require information to help them in their work, regardless of whether it is strategic or functional in nature.

Accordingly, the protection of information, and the security of systems which handle and process information, must also be of interest to managers.

This follows from a consideration of what constitutes both *strategy* and *strategic information*. We first note that planning is the method by which a person identifies key goals, and then how to achieve them. The person could be a junior worker deciding how to save money by choosing and buying cheaper sandwiches during a lunch break, or a senior manager making plans for a new business venture.

If the person is a senior manager considering goals for the entire organization, then *strategic planning* is being performed. Strategy refers to the development of broad scale and long-term designs for achieving objectives, as opposed to tactics which are designs for more focused and shorter-term objectives. *Strategic information* refers to knowledge or data that directly influences and affects the strategic planning process.

If the information is of high quality, of great reliability, relevant to the issues being considered, and available in sufficient detail when required, then it will be of extremely high value to the organization, owing to its contribution in helping improve the strategic planning process. Conversely, if the information does not meet these criteria, then at best the strategic planning process will be made more difficult.

This has ramifications for the long-term success of the organization in reaching its objectives. In the worst case, poor quality information can mislead or misinform during planning activities, with serious implications for the organization. It is imperative that strategic information is acquired, processed and provided in an optimum fashion. Appropriate and sufficient levels of security will be necessary for the information system to be able to fulfil this need.

Strategic information may be utilized by an organization for gaining competitive advantage because it is information that the entire organization and its members can apply or react to. If the application of that information is incorrect, or the information itself is incorrect, or even if the organization itself fails to make full use of the information, then the result could be that a competitor gains the advantage. This means that losing control over strategic information, or losing the information itself, can result in the loss of any organizational advantage that may otherwise be gained. Failing to use information, or allowing its use by a competitor, will markedly reduce the value of that information.

Industrial espionage

It is for this reason that the related issue of industrial espionage must also be considered by managers. At one time, it was a comparatively simple matter for management to take the responsibility for using or not using information. Today, however, the issue is complicated by the possibility of internal information being available to external organizations by use of industrial espionage techniques.

As a general rule of thumb, more than 85% of internal information can be obtained by outsiders using perfectly lawful methods such as researching newspapers, periodicals and texts. Information on new products may be slightly more difficult to obtain, but in many cases may be deduced from other sources.

A common example in the computer world involves sales people who are keen to 'hook' a potential buyer. In order to do this, they may drop hints about upcoming products or system characteristics. Another alternative is for technically competent staff to attend the many conferences or exhibitions promoting various products. Under the guise of being an interested buyer, they are often able to gain 'hands-on' access to the systems and information, often with the help of a willing but unsuspecting sales representative.

An industrial spy can collect data from a variety of sources, some lawful and acceptable, and others covert. In fact, covert sources are not always unlawful, and may not even be immoral; however, an organization which is found to utilize such methods would perhaps tarnish its reputation. It must be emphasised that use of covert methods could result in criminal or civil penalties for the parties involved.

Overt sources are openly and publicly available. Material in this category would include newspaper reports, specialist journals and books, speeches and papers, radio and television broadcasts, and court records. More detailed information could be obtained from market research and consultancy reports, financial statements and reports, stockbrokers research surveys, trade fairs, exhibits and brochures, and possibly detailed examination of a competitors' products. This latter source raises the issue of reverse engineering, which will be discussed in more detail in a later chapter.

Covert sources of information might be obtained following actions such as breaking into a competitor's property, bribing their suppliers or staff, putting one of your own staff into their organization, tapping into their data communication channels, and simple theft of plans or documents. Industrial espionage of this kind is a *very* serious matter, and should not be contemplated lightly. The author does not condone or encourage any such actions.

Organizations should always be alert to the possibility of external organizations attempting to use some or all of the above techniques against them. In particular, the fact that computer systems will store and process considerable quantities of data make them a key target for the industrial spy. The really determined spy would probably not bother with attempting to hack into a computer, as this approach is uncertain and unreliable. A much simpler method would be to steal the computer itself and then dissect the information it contains at leisure.

An example of this occurred in August 1991, when a thief stole a pre-release version of Lotus's 1-2-3 spreadsheet software from the offices of a British user group, only hours after it was first delivered. The thief crept undetected through three doors and five offices at the user group's premises, and escaped with a personal computer loaded with Lotus 1-2-3 for Windows and Ami Pro Version 2, an advanced word-processing package.

The danger of organizational dependencies

For most organizations, information is a key resource, perhaps almost a form of international currency. It is viewed as a commodity, with intrinsic value. The difficulty for modern organizations is that storing and processing large quantities of data is unwieldy and confusing without the appropriate tools. The speed, capacity and accuracy characteristic of computers becomes essential in providing for manipulation and cross-referencing of the data.

There may be little choice in utilizing the computer for data processing, and many organizations freely acknowledge a fundamental dependency upon IT. Indeed, the large quantities of data may preclude the possibility of manual or non-automatic manipulation: computer-based systems are almost mandatory for some functions within businesses, particularly large organizations. Examples include cataloguing or stock control, payroll, and budgeting functions; few staff would be willing to tackle these tasks without some form of computer assistance.

In a variety of ways, organizations are now dependent upon information and the information processing aspects of systems. For this reason, protection of the systems becomes a managerial issue, for which the responsibility cannot be delegated. Consideration of the issues at a high level within the business is particularly important because, unlike almost all other resources available to an organization, with the possible exception of time and money, information systems have a pervasive nature that permeates and affects the entire organization.

Even if an organization decides to fundamentally alter the nature of its information system, perhaps by removal of the system, it is a non-trivial task, especially if it is computer-based. This is because of the continually increasing dependency of the organization for the system to provide cost-effective storage capacity and sufficient data manipulation tools to identify, seek out, and retrieve key items or relationships between the data.

Despite the importance of computer systems, they often remain under the control of 'gurus' who have a predominantly technical perspective. Although the number of computer users is increasing, the number of people with the expertise and knowledge necessary to maintain and operate the systems in order to support the performance of business functions is actually *decreasing* as a proportion of the staff. Thus, the administration of a key resource is dependent upon the goodwill of a small and highly specialised team. This represents a threat in its own right.

Additionally, if computer technology is a major processing tool in an information system, an opportunity may exist for members of staff - or even someone with access from outside the organization - to gain control of the system. The system violator may then be able to turn the system to their own advantage. The presence of computers in information systems provides an additional opportunity for information misuse by people.

The threat of losing access to data can be very serious, even if the interruption is temporary. Many users assume that computer systems are reliable, and can provide continual service for the organization. Unfortunately, as experience eventually shows, this is not the case.

Reasons for management complacency

The difficulty that some managers have in addressing IT was highlighted in a survey carried out in the last quarter of 1991 by manufacturing analysts Benchmark Research, which reported that over a third of chief executives and directors in UK businesses approve expenditure on IT *simply in order to keep up with their competitors' investment in IT*, rather than for overall strategic reasons. Nearly half of the senior managers did not understand the ways in which IT can influence their businesses. The implication is that there is a great deal of work to do before managers begin to appreciate the implications of IT. It further suggests that a great deal of effort must be applied to ensure that the need for IT security is appreciated.

Paradoxically, part of the difficulty is that many managers, particularly at senior levels, are unable or unwilling to make use of computer systems themselves. This may be due to a minimum of training, perhaps because of lack of time; or alternatively because of a subconscious apprehension about technology. A survey of 1,500 members of the British Institute of Management was undertaken by the business journal *Management Today* and Microsoft. The results showed that 92% of managers were 'uncomfortable with computers'. The reasons were not so much due to fears about the hardware, but insufficient time to learn the systems (58%), or poor training or support (31%). Tellingly, 49% thought that there was considerable scope for improvement in the way that IT was used in their organization.

Organizations as a whole are surprisingly reluctant to recognise and deal with computer security threats. A major reason for this is that security failures are easily visible *after* the event. Before the event, however, reasons for obtaining and applying sufficient and adequate security measures can be difficult to justify. It is not easy to supply evidence that proves the need for security. By definition, suitable measures will succeed in preventing or constraining specific threats, and so losses that might otherwise arise from the threats can be difficult to quantify.

Not surprisingly, many organizations will assume that on a statistical basis, they are unlikely to be attacked, and on a probability per organization basis, the assumption is understandable. However, a number of factors may combine to dramatically modify the probability values. In particular, organizational publicity of almost any kind may draw unwelcome attention from an industrial spy, or from computer hackers. Examples of such publicity would include media articles about a new product, a major sales campaign, the winning of a large order, and even managerial pay rises. Any one of these can highlight the organization, and so change the probability of an attack.

Computer security myths

The perceived need for security may also be undermined due to a lack of managerial understanding or belief in the threats. Sometimes, this is the result of exaggeration in the reported cases. Indeed, an unfortunate trend has been for specific case studies to become more general and ultimately apocryphal in nature. The result is that a number of 'popular myths' have arisen.

One example is that computer-based information is more at risk than other kinds. Surveys carried out with victims and violators indicate that, in fact, more losses result from information obtained by word-of-mouth, insecure disposal of printed information, and simple observation. However, the publicity given to losses which derive from more 'glamorous' computer crimes seems to produce greater *awareness* of such threats.

Another example is the myth that a great deal of technical knowledge is required in order to commit a computer crime. In fact, the evidence that has been collected tends to suggest the opposite. Actual cases indicate that computers are also misused by people with minimal technical knowledge, but who are authorized to process data in a particular way.

In one case, an administrative clerk was responsible for approving expenses claims before they were entered into the computer for payment. She was able to introduce some false demands into the system by writing out and approving her *own* claims. In this way she indirectly instructed the computer to pay some expenses into her bank account. Although a computer crime had been committed, the clerk had no technical knowledge. Indeed, she never came into contact with any computer equipment because all of her work was paper-based.

A common assumption is that insiders from within the organization are the most serious threat to computer systems. Undoubtedly, this idea has some appeal. However, it must be realised that outsiders are much more difficult to trace and identify, although the results of their actions may be much easier to detect because they cannot possibly have the same in-depth knowledge of organizational routine.

By contrast, an insider is more likely to have a much better knowledge of the computer system, and so may be able to plan and cover his or her actions more easily. Despite this, insiders will be more exposed to detection as it is an on-going danger to them.

Accordingly, insiders will plan their actions much more carefully, and may also go for a bigger target to make their attack worthwhile. Nevertheless, it seems likely that insiders will be identified and caught more often, and as a consequence, will appear to be more of a risk to organizations.

In practice, however, we cannot say with any certainty that computer security violations *are* predominantly caused by insiders. What we *can* say is that of those violations which are detected, admitted by the organization, and the instigator identified; the majority *seem* to be caused by insiders.

Computer security threats could be caused by anyone with sufficient knowledge of an organization and, as we have seen from the discussion of industrial espionage, there are plenty of ways in which a prospective violator could acquire enough information to represent a threat.

Despite this, it is important to get deliberate computer security threats into their true perspective. This means that we must distinguish and hence exclude IT-related losses that do not actually arise from malevolent intent.

Just one example reported in 1990 concerns some astonishing figures from the US Defense Department. The figures detailed the final fate of IT systems, and are shown in table 7. If the percentages are translated into costs of software and hardware, it can be seen that without any harmful intent, a significant loss might be sustained by an organization.

Many of the threats attributed to hackers or viruses are actually due to entirely different causes. The most obvious example concerns loss of data, particularly from a PC. The publicity given to viruses that 'destroy data files' or 'interfere with programs' means that many users will immediately blame any peculiar events onto a virus.

Table 7: Final results for US Defense Department IT systems in 1990

Percentage of systems	Final destination of system
1.5%	Used as delivered
3%	Used, after modification
19%	Used, then abandoned
29%	'Vapourware' - paid for but never delivered
47.5%	Delivered, but never used.

Yet, in a surprisingly large number of cases, and some surveys put the figures in excess of 80%, the actual cause is user error, often compounded by ignorance or misuse of the system.

Faced with such confusing and sometimes inaccurate reporting, and an absence of hard facts, it is not surprising if managers in organizations are tempted to defer the subject of computer security.

Why managers must be involved

In many organizations, senior managers may deliberately choose to ignore technical matters, or alternatively delegate the responsibility to more technologically competent juniors.

In doing so they are losing control over their computer systems and, of course, their information resource. As a safety measure, they may require that regular management reports are produced, but this is inadequate for monitoring purposes, as it is very easy to hide potentially disastrous hazards under a blizzard of jargonistic 'techno-babble'.

Additionally, an environment is being created which encourages the difficulties to get worse. Managers become increasingly detached from technology, while their junior delegates continue to advance and apply their skills. The resulting divergence of perspective can be difficult to recombine.

In most cases, junior employees cannot possibly have the wide scale appreciation of the necessary detail that constitutes a fully operational organization. This is not a denigration of their role, however, as they are essential components in maintaining the smooth running of each of the functions that form the basis of the entire organization.

A breakdown in any one business function can quickly have detrimental effects in other operational activities. Poor performance by receptionist or switchboard operators can prevent customer enquiries from ever reaching the sales team. Success in organizations requires the continued cooperation and contribution of all staff at all levels.

Delegation of responsibility for computer systems to junior staff may be inappropriate. In the absence of managerial experience and guidance, it is not surprising if the junior resorts to applying only the technical skills which have proved successful in the past. But addressing computer security purely from a technological perspective inevitably minimises the opportunity for human aspects to be considered. Dealing with threats using technology alone avoids addressing the primary sources and causes of the threats. There is also danger in the assumption that technological protection mechanisms can be made to work correctly and reliably from the beginning.

Managers must recognise that addressing computer security issues is part of their responsibility, and cannot be delegated. They must focus upon getting the best from all the organizational resources, and this includes people *and* technology. Managers must learn to manipulate and control IT resources, balancing the facilities provided with the objectives of the organization.

Business objectives and computer security

Every organization will have a set of clearly defined primary goals or objectives. All activities performed by employees of the organization will be devoted to furthering progress towards those goals. It is counter-productive to justify any work which is not of direct contribution in improving performance of the necessary tasks.

Yet one of the great paradoxes of computers in business is the enormous number of organizations that fail to take sufficient account of computer systems when making their business plans. Despite the widely recognised advantages of information systems in improving co-ordination, marketing and customer-supplier communications; the nature and implications of systems are rarely included as key components in the grand plans of organizations.

This can result in a wide variety of difficulties, such as incompatible systems in different departments or divisions. Sometimes it may be possible to replace the discordant systems with a standard systems solution that can be applied on an organizational basis. In other cases, this may not be economically feasible.

However, such technological issues are almost trivial in comparison to the political and managerial problems of information systems. One of the most difficult tasks is identifying and seeking a consensus opinion on user requirements.

Agreement is almost impossible to achieve, as all parties will have a particular perspective that they will defend forcefully. If individual or local requirements are not met when a new system is introduced, that system will never be a success. Sometimes the requirements may be influenced by different national operating conditions; in other situations problems arise from incompatibilities with the actual tasks themselves.

Against this very general set of statements is the need for security mechanisms to be implemented, but with the proviso that they should not conflict with the achievement of objectives. It would be contrary to overall business objectives if security measures which are intended to increase the reliability of a computer system, were actually to reduce the ease of use or effectiveness with which the system could be applied to performing tasks.

Nevertheless, the security measures must prevent, or at the very least, severely constrain, any factors which would serve as system inhibitors or sources of threat. If these threats are not dealt with, they can interfere with the successful operation and utilization of the systems.

An optimum balance point is desirable between the constraining features of security mechanisms and the need for an optimised environment within which to perform necessary tasks. This is often expressed as a relationship between security of a system and its ease of use. The more secure a system is made, the less easy it may be for anyone to use. Correspondingly, the easier a system is to use, the less security can be applied to it. The ideal balance point can be identified as the circumstances under which the greatest level of threat prevention can be implemented with least inconvenience and expenditure for the organization.

However, this point cannot be predicted in advance or with great precision. In many cases, it may only be determined by the use of on-going experimentation techniques to see which security features are acceptable both to the users and to those who are responsible for securing the system.

Unfortunately, using an experimental approach alone can lead to weaker security than is appropriate, because some threats to systems are rare. In the absence of observable danger to the system, there will be a temptation to neglect or cut-back on security against such threats. When measures are removed or modified for this reason, they may be devalued in the eyes of users. Eventually this can result in insufficient security and complacency by the users. The organization will then be at its weakest, and threats to computer security become more likely.

Costing computer security

An important step in addressing security is to establish how much the various mechanisms will cost to implement. At the same time, estimates can be made of the losses that the organization could suffer if appropriate security measures were *not* put into place.   These various measures are then compared to determine whether the suggested methods and levels of security are cost-effective against any losses.

The computers and their instructions also have a value in themselves. The precision and performance of the hardware affects the timeliness and quality of information. Instructions can be entered into the system to control the input, processing and output activities.   These may be used to perform normal administrative functions or directly modify data. Thus, if the system or its instructions are faulty or in error, there is the possibility that flaws or inaccuracies will occur, and so pose the threat of serious losses for the organization.

It is possible for someone inside the organization to recognise how these instructions may be reapplied, misused or misdirected. It may be tempting for an individual to take advantage of loopholes in the system for personal gain. A variety of techniques for misusing computer systems underlie many cases of fraud or of industrial espionage, where organizational data such as design or construction plans would be extremely useful to a competing organization.

Naturally, each of the possible threats to information systems will have a certain degree of probability associated with them. Some threats are more likely than others. While it is impossible to predict the likelihood of threats occurring with great accuracy, it does not prevent specialists from making estimates, often using one of the following three methods:

- Use observed results from a larger population. Although it is impossible to predict if or when a house may be burgled, national statistics may be used to calculate how many houses will be burgled in a year, and to calculate the average loss per burglary. These sorts of calculations are carried out continually by insurance firms, and similar calculations are performed by equipment manufacturers with regard to machine lifetimes. In a similar fashion, some trade unions carry out surveys on human error rates as work time increases, and this can be used to estimate error probabilities.
- Use observed results from the specific system. The system itself could also be used to provide on-going statistical information regarding a variety of events.
- Use a consensus approach. Here, a group of experts or consultants may be requested to provide their own estimates, and a consensus achieved when the values - possibly following debate or argument - are reasonably consistent.

Using the above techniques, it may be possible to arrive at a reasonable figure for the losses that could be incurred by the organization following a successful attack against computer systems. The next stage would be to identify mechanisms that can provide protection against such attacks, or at least minimise the damage that could ensue.

Unfortunately, some security specialists have resorted to other rather dubious methods for estimating the value of losses that can occur. This results in predictions along the lines of 'current growth suggests that by the year X, computer-related losses will be Y millions'. The claims are often very large and could be extremely worrying if taken at face value.

Many of these claims assume that the growth of the threat will remain constant and unchecked - a highly unlikely event. Furthermore, they fail to take account of the effect of people and the self-governing properties of some systems. As the threats and the losses that they can cause become greater and more common, so awareness - and hence the incentive to adopt suitable counter-measures - increases.

For any given instance of a threat, the amount of danger to an organization will change as time passes. Initially, the danger from a specific threat is fairly low. Subsequently, as other organizations suffer from the threat, or similar problems, the risk of the organization suffering from the threat increases.

At a certain critical point, the publicity and general awareness of the threat is sufficient to begin to influence the probability of risk. Appropriate protection measures are being installed by organizations against that particular threat, and so the risk decreases.

However, it must be remembered that once it has been identified, a threat can never be entirely eliminated. The continuing success of the security measures is dependent upon the protection mechanisms being continued and maintained at optimum levels. Thus the existence of each threat initiates a self-governing process which may be accommodated at the discretion of the organization.

As an aside, it is interesting to observe that many of the figures for losses or threats are publicised by commercial firms that have an interest in promoting a service or perhaps a product that will 'deal' with the particular threat under consideration.

The reality is that, with a very few exceptions, it is *impossible* to put any meaningful figure onto the value of computer security losses. Only in a few *very* special cases with extensive documentation, can credence be given to such values. The cases normally refer to losses that are incurred by organizations which are obliged to report precisely the amounts involved. The organizations would usually be publicly-accountable bodies, such as government departments, and so reasonably accurate values may be expected and hopefully obtained from their records.

In almost all other cases, a limited number of examples are taken by the evaluating body, and an extrapolation performed to produce a figure which supposedly represents national or industry sector losses from computer theft, or fraud, or computer viruses, or whatever the report focuses upon. Such figures should be viewed with healthy scepticism.

Identifying the options

When dealing with computer security matters, managers may wish to seek external advice. External consultants or suppliers could be invited to suggest products or mechanisms that would provide suitable levels of protection against the identified threats. The cost of the consultants, their tools, and their effectiveness in dealing with the various threats must then be established, and compared with the cost of not doing anything, as described earlier.

This has a number of advantages and disadvantages. In practice, there are two options for managers wishing to utilize external resources. The first is to retain responsibility for security within the organization, but to draw upon outside experts for more information and advice. The second is to recognise the limitations of internal facilities and expertise, and therefore to offload some or all of the responsibility to an independent, external organization.

Advice may be provided by a commercial organization, such as a consultancy group, or by seeking opinions from academics. Academic experts have the advantage of being less likely to exhibit bias in favour of a particular product or service, but their interest in the work will often be from a theoretical perspective.

The scholarly viewpoint taken is not necessarily going to be the best one for an organization seeking solutions to their problems. Some academics have a reputation for treating consultancy work of this kind as an excellent opportunity to collect data for case studies. This can mean that the academic has no real incentive to provide a solution, as any outcome from the work is simply material for the case portfolio.

Therefore, while academics may be useful in providing an impartial analysis of the problem, some of them may not be suitable for going beyond that point and providing detailed advice and, in particular, they may not be available on a long-term basis.

The alternative is to employ a commercial consultancy firm. These firms will have experts who are in a better position to have more experience of the commercial aspects of the issues they address, although that does not necessarily mean that they will actually *have* the experience.

Some organizations have found that commercial consultancy businesses may not always provide the desired expertise. There is a possibility that bids for business will be presented by senior partners with genuine expertise in the field, but all subsequent work will be carried out by more junior consultants, for whom the project may be their first real assignment. Even with senior levels of supervision, the client firm will be depending on the competence of the junior staff.

Nevertheless, no matter how junior or inexperienced the consultant, the commercial background to the firm means that the expert will have an interest in providing good service over an extended period. Poor work will rapidly result in a very bad reputation which will immediately undermine the quality of future bids for work.

The most common reason that organizations are wary of commercial consultants is the possibility that their advice may be incorrect or inappropriate, not least as a result of the consultant being unable to understand the subtle nuances of the client business thoroughly. Clearly, no outsider can have such a good understanding of the business of the organization, and the way that departments and functions interact, as the resident staff.

Despite this, given the wide-ranging skills of a suitably experienced consultant, there is no reason why the expert cannot provide extremely high-quality advice that may not be available from any other source. However, there are four other possible reasons why an organization may be wary of employing a consultancy.

Firstly, there is the possibility that to utilize an external consultancy represents an admission of failure. This need not be the case, as there will be many organizations which do not have all the necessary expertise available in-house, especially if it is experience of a kind that is very rarely required during the normal business activities. Small organizations in particular would not be expected to have the relevant internal resources.

The second reason is the fear that calling upon consultants will cost too much. There is little doubt that for long-term work, consultancy rates may appear to be very expensive, and it may be more cost-effective to employ contractors or fixed-term staff. However, the client organization may consider it appropriate and even attractive to take wide-ranging action by addressing several issues at the same time.

For example, this could entail a thorough check of plans for disaster recovery, security and contingency policies, and even reviewing IT audit procedures. By taking advantage of the extensive work required, and perhaps even economic climate conditions such as a recession, it may be possible to negotiate substantial discounts in consultancy fees.

The third reason concerns the fact that some consultancies are notorious for encouraging what is termed 'client-dependency'. This is where a client organization becomes dependent upon the services provided by the consultancy. Once the consultant gets access to the organization, it may be possible for them to expand the job profile, resulting in more work over a longer timescale. Naturally, the client should be aware of the danger, and strenuously resist it. The best defence is to have a clear understanding of what is required, and formally define the boundaries of the work.

The final fear is that use of a consultancy may reveal weaknesses unnecessarily. This relates to the client-dependency problem, but also refers to the fact that using an external body to examine aspects of your organization is, by definition, 'opening yourself up' for very close scrutiny by outsiders. No matter what contracts and guarantees are put in place, at the end of the day the consultants are working for themselves, and not for the customer organization.

Managerial approaches to deal with computer security

In the light of the analysis of the possible threats to systems, the organizational representatives may then make one of four possible decisions on what to do about the identified threats.

Prevent the possibility of the threat   In order to prevent the threat from occurring, it may be possible to modify or remove certain of the system functions which otherwise provide loopholes or weaknesses.   It may be considered more cost-effective to reduce the system capabilities in order to eliminate the possibility of some threats.

An example might be to remove any possibility of access to a computer system from outside the organization.   This would have the advantage of preventing hackers from attempting to break in, but might also cause difficulties for authorized users, such as sales representatives, who might have a perfectly good reason for seeking remote access to a centralised system.

A management decision will almost certainly be required if the measures necessary to prevent the threat would require a change to the operational practices of the organization.

Install measures to control the threat   Another approach might be to apply a number of protective measures to help control and limit the opportunity for threats in such a way that the occurrence of the threat will result in bearable losses.   Examples of possible measures suitable for this approach include:

- Cryptography.
- Secure operating and communication systems.
- Secure development strategies and standards.
- Identification and authentication mechanisms.
- Database access and reliability controls.
- Multi-level security domains.
- Network and physical controls.

Common sense should be applied in selecting measures. A heavy-duty locked door may be a simpler and more cost-effective mechanism than complex technology-based access controls. It would also provide more protection against other threats, such as fires.

Transfer the loss that results from a threat In the third approach, the system itself remains unchanged, but the loss that would occur in the event of a threat is transferred to another organization. Some losses arising from threats can be transferred in this way, at a premium, through various types of insurance. While this approach may not be suitable for all threats, it can be extremely cost-effective for more unusual but nevertheless devastating sources of threat, such as earthquakes.

Retain the threat In the final approach, the organization decides to do nothing and therefore must accept whatever consequences result from computer system breakdown. This may be because the cost of the prevention or protection mechanism is more than the cost of the threat.

In many cases, organizations will be well acquainted with this approach, as it is encountered whenever a new product or service is launched. If the launch is a failure, the loss must be borne by other organizational resources. For this approach to be viable, the threats must be small-scale and of comparatively minor cost to the organization.

Applying the options

Even with internal expertise or external advice, the organization still may not consider it cost-effective to try to deal with the difficulties of running a computer-based information system, quite apart from addressing the threats to computer security.

A decision may be taken to offload part or all of the responsibility for computer systems to an external organization. This may be referred to as Facilities Management or FM. FM which is concerned specifically with computer services is often referred to as Outsourcing, although the two concepts are distinct.

In general, facilities management refers to a wide variety of organization-independent tasks. The term FM has been used for all of the following services: contract cleaning, catering, landscaping, mechanical and electrical engineering, building fabrics, space planning, communications, security, relocation, information technology, energy, general maintenance, fleet management, and even interior design.

Outsourcing refers to the decision to contract out part or all of the running of the computer system to an outside organization. In contrast to FM, strategic management responsibilities for the computer services generally remain within the organization. Outsourcing has several clear advantages over retaining the computer services function within the organization.

- Skills which do not exist within the user company, or would take time to develop, can be bought in.
- Full accountability can be established. There can be few managers who would not welcome the prospect that someone else has the responsibility when things go wrong.
- Putting an external agency in charge of the day-to-day running of the system will free technical personnel for more pressing work and non-technical managers to concentrate on the jobs that they are paid to do.
- Cost savings and other efficiencies may result.

However, outsourcing is not a straightforward option. The biggest problem that organizations will face is determining which operational responsibilities to delegate out and which to retain. Certainly, few organizations would be complacent at the thought of handing over the running of their systems in their entirety, and most IT managers will not want to do themselves out of a job.

Although the burden of securing a system could be taken on by the outsourcing organization, this raises issues of confidentiality and security when external people have access to organizational information. Furthermore, if the decision is taken to utilize an outsourcing agency, there will always be a worry over what happens if the outsourcing organization subsequently goes out of business.

Most outsourcing firms will point out that their objective is to supplement rather than supplant in-house services. In other words, they take care of operational aspects of computer system management, and leave the strategic side to the customer. However, it is difficult to see how practical guidelines could be developed for this division of responsibility.

One clear advantage of outsourcing, however, would be that both the internal computer services department and the end-users would have someone else to complain about. Although apparently flippant, the statement suggests a measure of internal harmony that could be very valuable.

Management of security

Management skills are fundamental to addressing the threats to computer and data security. People make mistakes and errors, and managers must spend part of their time dealing with such problems in order to minimise the effect they would otherwise have on the organization. Ideally, steps are taken to ensure that the problems do not occur again in the future. These same principles can and should be applied to IT security.

Managers addressing functional and strategic issues will have to understand not only the need for computer security measures, but also recognise the value of active support and promotion of the measures. Furthermore, the managers themselves must be seen to comply with the measures in full.

Managers may not bear this responsibility alone. One way of addressing security threats is for end users to be educated to think in terms of the greater good, not only for themselves, but for their colleagues and the organization as a whole. Thus security would be a shared responsibility and built into employee attitudes.

With this perspective, we could move into the more philosophical domain of ethical considerations. However, this may not be helpful. Some would argue that recognising ethical obligations is a voluntary action, and that it is difficult to measure the *actual* value to an organization of ethical behaviour. For other organizations, particularly some large multi-nationals, ethical issues are considered important enough to be incorporated into their 'mission statements'. The value and contribution of ethics to a problem remains a matter for managerial discretion.

If ethical behaviour is in a sense voluntary, then its mandatory counterpart may well be formal legislation. It is not possible to be precise about the extent to which legislation is of benefit in helping or encouraging greater computer security within organizations. Surveys indicate that some organizations are not assisted by legislation, although this may be because legislation is not perceived as actively contributing anything; indeed it may even be viewed as intrusive or a serious constraint. This is likely to be a problem of perception.

Underlying all of the above issues are two key themes: cooperation and communication. All those people involved in contributing to the organization, from the part-time cleaner to the chairman of the board, must be aware of the essential role that they play. Understanding of roles and their contribution to the organization is built upon awareness and involvement. In a similar way, the objectives of computer security should be communicated. The danger is that to do so may be to expose the organization to precisely those same threats that it is trying to avoid.

In practice, the security of computer-based information systems is not actually a difficult task. The threats to security are, in general, clear cut and well understood. By far the majority of threats that an organization is ever likely to encounter have already been experienced by other organizations, and the effects they have had, and the methods for dealing with them should therefore be very well documented. Furthermore, each example of a threat will almost certainly have more than one possible solutions, although naturally they will vary in cost and effectiveness.

The difficulty for organizations concerns the actual *implementation* of solutions by security specialists, by managers, and by organizational staff. Putting security mechanisms into place, and the subsequent effects of those measures upon the organization, are major issues that can have substantial implications for the strategies and success of the organization.

It is true that computer systems can fail for a number of reasons, whether by poor system design or implementation, or by simple hardware failure. However, for such threats, the use of appropriate backup mechanisms and the availability of reserve systems - which need not always be computer-based, although this will be increasingly necessary - are part of the standard precautions.

But when people are added into the picture, security mechanisms may not be straightforward. As soon as mechanisms are used, they will affect what people do. The way in which the mechanisms are applied will also be influenced by the attitudes and ideas of their users. The main difficulty for security specialists is in trying to help management and other organizational staff appreciate the nature of security threats.

This means communicating the fact that *people* are at the heart of the problem, not the technology. It is people who misuse the systems. It is people who prevent systems from working. It is people who are responsible for poor software or hardware designs. It is people who are responsible for not bothering with today's backup of data, or for not checking that the backup data can actually be retrieved if it became necessary. The message is that people are the first, last and main lines of defence against computer security violations, because people form the foundation of most serious security threats. User considerations are therefore imperatives which merit separate consideration, and will be discussed in the next chapter.

Summary

Managers play a fundamental role in determining the effectiveness of computer security measures. In their role as leaders and planners they must identify sources of threats, the probability of those threats occurring, the cost of countermeasures, the selection of countermeasures, and finally the promotion of compliance with countermeasures.

Managers must be seen to be bound by security mechanisms at least as much as other employees. Without that compliance, the security measures will not be taken seriously, and in the best case will then be rendered ineffective against the threats. In the worst case, a half-hearted attention to security can suggest that a similarly gentle approach will be taken with any transgressions, and this is *not* a message that managers should communicate to their staff.

In dealing with security issues, managers must be aware of user requirements and perspectives. Seemingly pointless rules and regulations will be disregarded, while careful explanation of decisions is more likely to result in understanding and compliance. User issues are therefore of key importance in improving security in general, and computer security in particular.

5 Spreading the message

- **User requirements**
- **The need for training and policy dissemination**
- **Promoting internal awareness**
- **The twin-edged sword: external and media publicity**
- **Taking responsibility for spreading the message**
- **Dealing with transgressions**
- **Summary**

In this chapter, we consider some user aspects of computer security. It is important to take into account the preferences and requirements of the user. This is because one of the major headaches for a security specialist is not, in reality, the difficulty of trying to secure a system. Instead, it is the problem of trying to ensure that the security mechanisms are *understood* and *implemented* by those who could otherwise do a lot of damage by non-compliance.

One of the reasons for non-compliance with security procedures could be due to genuine ignorance or non-comprehension of what is required. However, this will be of little consolation or help after the security breakdown has occurred.

Complicating the matter further, for many organizations, is the fear that wide publicity of security measures not only undermines their effectiveness, but may also suggest methods by which systems can be bypassed.

User requirements

When an information system is first made available to users, the expectation is that the system will be used to improve the efficiency and effectiveness of the user's work. Indeed, many of the characteristics of the system will have been designed by taking into account business and departmental objectives, practical implementation considerations, and perhaps even suggestions from users.

Once the system has been used for some time, user perceptions may change. Some of the functions provided will be essential to the user, while there may be others which are not required. Normally, these can be completely ignored.

However, extreme frustration can be caused if the functions that are supposed to be provided by a system are suddenly unavailable, or do not operate in the way described in documentation or in training courses. Deviations in the expected patterns of system behaviour make it unpredictable, or worse, unreliable. If the users are dependent upon the system for performing a task, a great deal of conflict can be generated when the users are prevented from doing so through no fault of their own.

Distinguishing between availability and reliability

One of the most difficult ideas to communicate to users and system developers is that there is a distinction between availability and reliability. Many developers tend to assume that they mean the same thing. The Oxford English Dictionary (2nd Edition) of 1989 defines availability as:

> 'The quality of being available; capability of being employed or made use of'

By contrast, reliability is defined as:

> 'The quality of being reliable'

In turn, reliable is defined as:

> 'That may be relied upon; in which reliance or confidence may be put; trustworthy, safe, sure'

These definitions are rather too general; we require more relevance to computer systems, and security in particular. Suitably focused definitions appear in the glossary of the McGraw-Hill publication Datapro Reports on Information Security, dated January 1991, which describes availability as:

> 'The degree to which data is where it is required, when it is required, and in the form in which it is required, by the user'

Similarly, the definition of reliability is given as:

> 'Dependability of a system to perform in a specified way without making error'

The relevance of making this distinction is that many system developers confuse the two definitions, and attempt to provide availability by implementing reliability. Sometimes, this may be by using so-called 'fault-tolerant' or 'non-stop' computer hardware.

Yet in some cases, users require availability, but not necessarily reliability. For example, in a local area network consisting of several personal computers, it is not necessary to have 100% reliability in all computers. Even if one computer breaks down, all the others remain usable. Thus availability is maintained.

A practical example of the difference concerns immigration control at airports. Immigration officers have the task of checking that an applicant is not on a list of several thousand names identifying known terrorists and assassins. These checks must be performed 24 hours a day, 7 days a week, every week of the year. There must never be a situation where the appropriate check cannot be performed.

This means that the list of names must *continually* be *available* to the officers. It does not mean that any one system used for the checking process must be *reliable*, although this is clearly a desirable objective.

Policing systems

Confusing availability and reliability suggests a poor understanding of the requirements of a system. The result can be the production of an unsuitable system, and dissatisfied users. In a comparable way, difficulties may arise if it appears that seemingly non-essential or non-contributory functions are given a higher priority, perhaps to the detriment of other 'more important' features. But when the functions are concerned with implementing security, and so cannot be ignored, the conflict of interest may become more significant. Security which intrudes upon the normal operations of the system, so far as a user is concerned, can breed resentment.

Some users may be concerned at the 'policing' nature of security measures. The fear for users is that the supervisory nature of the functions can be misused. This can occur when the functions are applied not for workplace monitoring, but for workplace *performance* monitoring.

A simple example is the use of computers to record the number of key-presses per hour, which enables the monitoring of work carried out by data-entry clerks. Any clerk who consistently falls below a certain rate of data-entry, or fails to improve standards, may be dismissed from employment. The original purpose of the monitoring tool may have been something as simple as detecting if a computer was being used outside normal working hours and, therefore, possibly being used by an unauthorized individual.

From users to abusers

The presence of discontent, for reasons such as those highlighted above, can be the basis of users starting to rebel against the organization and its systems. This rebellion may become manifest in several ways.

Earlier, we drew a distinction between the insider and the outsider. Analysis of contrasts such as these may be of value in helping us to identify potential sources of threat. In particular, it may be possible to identify suitable counter-measures to the penetration techniques that would be used by the various categories of system violator.

Unfortunately, it is not so easy to identify the sort of people against whom security measures are aimed. It is quite likely that the people who carry out fraudulent activities or who commit computer crimes seem to be perfectly average. There is no guarantee that they will be intelligent or well-educated, or in any way unusual.

In almost all cases where identification has been possible, the people responsible for computer misuse are ordinary people, who have simply taken advantage of a specific opportunity, or are inflicting some form of retribution upon the organization.

It is possible for us to distinguish three main categories of people who may be involved in some form of computer crime or system penetration.

Opportunists

Many computer crimes are committed by people who originally had no intention of making a habit of such acts. They may have perhaps detected a weakness in a system and, as a result of greed or discontent, have decided to exploit it. They may start by simple misuse of ordinary resources in a similar way to most of their colleagues. They may write personal letters and post them using the business postal system. Often, they will make personal telephone calls. While apparently trivial, abuses of this kind can begin to accumulate and so foster a less responsible attitude to the organization and its resources.

Before long, the person may start to try out more wide-ranging schemes for obtaining more expensive resources, perhaps as unofficial perks. Alternatively, as the employee is promoted, or gains access to more valuable resources, the opportunity for a major abuse can arise. Where computer systems are involved, there is rarely any point in small-scale misuse, except perhaps for playing computer games. Eventually, the opportunist may decide to risk everything on a major computer crime.

A characteristic of the actions of an opportunist is that they are almost invariably one-off, and there will be little in the manner or constitution of the person that offers any warning of the impending problem.

Hackers and terminal junkies

More problematic for the specialist are more dedicated people for whom system penetration or programming is their hobby or pseudo-profession. Hackers are differentiated from straightforward opportunists mainly by the single-minded repetition of the computer system penetration attempts and, according to some claims, the absence of any malevolence. They may be trying to prove their skills by breaking into ever more secure systems. It is popularly believed that hackers will be highly intelligent boys, perhaps university or sixth-form students, who delight in simply trying to break into systems. However, studies carried out in this area suggest that, where they are found, women hackers will be just as proficient. By contrast, terminal junkies, sometimes called whiz-kids, are generally considered to be more benevolent individuals who can solve 'any computing problem' and who have not so far attempted a hack.

These people are often thought to be loners, socialising only with other like-minded individuals, preferably using electronic mail or an equivalent. They will often have difficulty seeing hacking or computer penetration as being any form of offence, as no perceivable damage is done. In practice, hacking can result in significant damage through misdirected resources or workload modifications. Therefore, in many countries, hacking is viewed as a very serious threat, with correspondingly severe penalties; authorities are often hampered, however, by the youth of the offenders, even assuming that they can be identified.

Specialists

These are dedicated people who thoroughly understand the potential gains that can be had from computer crime. Typically, they will be computer professionals who have chosen to follow a high-risk, high-profit route by applying industrial espionage techniques for information acquisition purposes.

A popular newspaper belief is that there are occasions where such people apply their skills for government 'approved' activities. A common example quoted is espionage, although not of the industrial variety. Alternatively, it may be suggested that such specialists are employed in order to destabilise various organizations for subversive, political or economic ends. However, no substantial evidence for this has been located.

From the point of view of information systems, the two extremes of computer crime carried out by specialists could range from straightforward theft of systems or data, for investigation at leisure, through to more advanced forms of electronic eavesdropping, perhaps using the TEMPEST principles described in chapter one.

The need for training and policy dissemination

Individuals interpret their circumstances in different ways from day to day. On one particular day they may feel sufficiently motivated to abuse a computer system. This continually changing perspective cannot be incorporated into the design of a technological system because it is a social or psychological issue. Therefore, computer threats that arise as a result of such disgruntled employees cannot be dealt with as part of the fundamental technological structure of the system itself.

Sometimes, the opportunities for problems to occur may unwittingly be supplied by the organization itself. A good example of this concerns the provision of information about a system. The more complex an information system is, the greater the likelihood that extensive documentation will be necessary to use the system. This documentation, or at least a substantial subset of it, will normally be available to users.

In many cases, a great deal of user documentation is provided as manuals in or near user-accessible computer rooms, even if the exact same documentation is already available on-line from within the computer system itself. Although this can be justified on the grounds that it means users do not have to use the computer system to study the documentation, it also means that people who are not authorized users may be able to obtain information about the system.

Indeed, it was precisely this problem that lay behind the theft of some manuals for Pacific Bell's COSMOS system in 1981. COSMOS, the Computer System for Mainframe Operations, was a database program used by local telephone companies. Access to the manuals for this system would enable so-called phone 'phreaks' to indulge in their 'hobby' for disrupting the telephone system.

Even if paper-based documentation is not available, someone gaining access to the on-line help system will frequently be given considerable assistance by the computer. For example, the on-line help will contain examples and suggestions on how to proceed with a particular task, with cross-references to related information. Surprisingly, while specific users and applications may be assigned to security domains, the on-line help is rarely domain-sensitive and, furthermore, is not often found to be context-sensitive.

This means that, in theory, it would be possible for someone to gain access to documentation which provides direct or indirect information on how to bypass or compromise security measures. The details do not necessarily have to relate to actual security mechanisms.

For example, it is often very useful to be able to recover a data file that was accidentally deleted. The same procedures may also be used, in some circumstances, to retrieve material that was *intentionally* deleted to prevent disclosure. This weakness does not apply to all systems, but it nevertheless highlights that documentation on procedures for performing perfectly reasonable actions may be applied to other, unauthorized, actions.

Clearly, such potentially revealing material should not be left available for just anyone to access. This also applies to more general material, which should be restricted according to the actual 'need to know'. It may be useful for organizations to develop and promote a mindset where there is no such thing as a 'safe' document for public access.

Computer information systems are rarely appropriate for use by complete beginners. Instead, new users must be trained in the use of the system. This training will be an on-going process and, at first, the users will be encouraged to improve their skills and expertise *within the domain of their responsibilities*. However, subsequent to this, the increasing expertise and opportunity for users to learn more will encourage them to explore beyond their domains. This desire for progression may be contrary to the requirements of the organization. Yet it is an inherent property derived from computer systems and human nature that some users will wish to advance in this manner.

Some organizations will actively seek and hire new employees with prior computer experience and enthusiasm for high technology, and yet this *must* increase the security threats eventually encountered, both in terms of the potential for occurrence and the actual severity of any event which occurs. The inclination to explore the limits of systems may be very helpful in advancing an individual's knowledge, but it is *also* likely to be contrary to the requirements of the organization. The computer enthusiast is likely to lose interest in seemingly mundane applications of computers, and will be tempted to use the system as an extension to his hobby.

We have seen that technology alone cannot provide a suitable solution to the security problems of organizations. They must also have support and understanding from the users themselves, be they the most junior clerks or the most senior board members. In order to achieve this support and understanding, there must be a set of mechanisms for training in security issues and subsequent promotion of awareness throughout the organization. The training must obviously reflect technological issues, but in the context of the social and security requirements of the organization and its staff.

Many organizations will implement a form of initiation or induction to the organization. At the smaller end of the scale, this may be as simple as a quick tour of the office and an introduction to colleagues. At the larger end of the scale, there may be a series of formal presentations by representatives from various departments, explaining their functions and possibly the relationships between them. Regardless of the nature or scope of the presentations, the common theme is to provide the orientation and socialisation mechanisms that a new employee requires at the start of a new job. Four main areas are normally addressed:

- General information necessary for the employee to perform his or her daily tasks.
- An introduction to the organization, its history, goals and general activities.

- The contribution that the employee can make for the benefit of the organization.
- Information about policies, rules and financial details.

The policies and structure of the organization may be enshrined in the contractual obligations of all employees and this, at least, has the advantage of providing the organization with grounds for action in the event of non-compliance. However, if the employment contract is the sole statement of security requirements, there is a danger that employees will lose their awareness of the issues. At best, such contracts are read once upon receipt and to confirm details such as pay, holiday entitlement, and so on. Thereafter, the paperwork will be filed and largely forgotten.

A common alternative is to include a clause in the employment contract to the effect that the employee must observe all *current* security obligations as a condition of employment. This has the advantage of allowing flexibility, but the disadvantage that the organization *must* take every opportunity to ensure sufficient awareness by all employees. All too often, new conditions of work or policies are issued to employees either by a generalised announcement which appears on public notice boards (often recognised by the complete absence of staff reading them), or by memos or letters sent through internal mail to each member of staff.

The notice-board approach has the disadvantage that it may actually serve to publicise security weaknesses. Conversely, the use of an individual memo enables the reader to be targeted much more effectively than a generalised public message, but may suffer from being just one of.the many internal messages or memos that are submitted on a daily basis for the attention of employees. A more effective means is required for the urgency of security to be satisfactorily communicated.

Nevertheless, it is crucial to communicate the necessary ideas in a fashion which can be optimised for specific requirements. One way would be to use existing procedures for on-going training and development programmes, extending them to incorporate security awareness as a major component.

It is appropriate to draw a distinction between training and development. Training refers to the provision and maintenance of skills required to perform *current* tasks, while development refers to skills that may be required in *future* jobs or tasks.

Therefore, training sessions could be used to address current computer security problems and the mechanisms for dealing with them; while development sessions could be used for consideration of future issues, and the prevention of security problems.

In much the same way that staff can be trained in customer issues, and internal procedures, so the problems of computer security could also be discussed. It is not necessary to go into detail about the nature of the security mechanisms themselves, but rather to provide an overview of the threats and how the mechanisms *help* to deal with them. Practical demonstrations and case studies are comparatively easy to set up and use, and can be extremely effective in highlighting the dangers to computers.

The opportunity could also be taken to identify characteristics that often indicate the possibility of computer threats, for example colleagues experiencing depression or frustration at some aspect of their work. Results from the training sessions could be fed back into later meetings, along with additional information on topical matters.

Promoting internal awareness

Once the level of awareness has been raised, the next difficulty concerns how to proceed with *maintaining* the appreciation of security issues within the organization. A fashionable approach, using drinking mugs with themes or posters or pens, may be appropriate for encouraging increases in quality or customer awareness, but may not be so well suited to the critical tasks of communicating messages that are of fundamental importance to the continuing operations of the organization. There are two main dangers that any campaign must avoid.

The first is the possibility that one particular approach may appear to trivialise a possibly sensitive issue. Use of cartoon figures spouting clichés suggests a frivolous technique which contrasts and conflicts with the need for serious consideration of the issues.

The second danger is that of the audience's suffering boredom or becoming insensitive or unresponsive to the message, following earlier overexposure to similar awareness campaigns. Quite apart from a tendency to ignore information that does not directly relate to jobs, even the most diligent of staff may fail to notice minor changes in existing procedures or policies if they appear only in memos buried within other information.

The unusual nature of computer security, compared with many other organizational issues, means that a careful and considered approach must be taken to promoting awareness. It is important to recognise that security awareness can form *part* of the regular training and development of all staff members. At reasonably regular intervals, staff development courses could be held for briefing on relevant matters.

These courses would provide an opportunity for current security procedures and policies, among other things, to be examined by those who must apply them. In particular, any changes or differences from previous policies - no matter how minor - should be clearly highlighted and justified.

The use of the word 'examined' is deliberate. The object of the briefing should be to ensure that, as part of the process, staff consider *why* any procedures or policies are in their current form. A simple statement of fact may be sufficient in some cases, but will inevitably undermine the depth of awareness within individuals.

Conversely, a detailed consideration is likely to be more successful in communicating the message. In other words, there must be sufficient presentation of information for staff to understand not just the policies, but also more general aspects of the issues that inspired the policies.

This means that the organization must have a degree of trust in its employees. Staff should be presented not only with the methods for dealing with threats, but with a basic knowledge of the threats themselves. This knowledge can be used to explain why security measures are necessary, and the effects of both compliance and non-compliance. The opportunity could be taken to illustrate that computer security concerns a variety of issues.

For example, in addition to simple protection of data by taking full and adequate backups, and keeping those backups safe and secure in their own right, security also refers to the overall working environment of the organization. Unaccompanied strangers should *always* be challenged. Doors and filing cabinets should *always* be secured - if they cannot be made safe, then sensitive material should never be left in them. Doors should never be wedged open, and doors that require security passes should never be held open for anyone.

Any potential threat should never be ignored for someone else to deal with. Great emphasis should be put on the fact that security is not just for the benefit of the organization, but also has direct effects upon all of its customers, suppliers and employees.

Giving this information to the employee should not compromise the security of the organization. An employee should only be in a particular job position if he or she is trusted for that level of responsibility. This means that the information provided about security issues should reflect the level of trust invested in the employee for the current time, and that will apply at least until the next employee review.

At the same time, it should be made clear to all staff at all levels that any decisions or actions taken by a member of staff for *justifiable* reasons of security will never be punished. This is because there will inevitably be 'grey areas' in interpreting what is, and what is not, allowed.

There can be few junior members of staff who have not, at some time in their career, been requested or instructed by a senior person to perform a task that they suspect or know is contrary to regulations. Examples would include secretaries photocopying journals or books, and computer users lending or borrowing software for short-term use.

It is essential that an organizational mindset is developed and promoted whereby policies and the law are not compromised. This process will be aided if staff do not fear that they will be penalised for correct, but sometimes socially distasteful, actions, such as reporting blatant piracy of software. At the moment, illegal copying of software is tolerated in some organizations by surprisingly senior people, and it may be some time before a more appropriate mindset develops.

The twin-edged sword: external and media publicity

Related to the problem of internal awareness is the effect of external or media publicity. A slight distinction may be drawn between the two forms. External publicity refers to threats specific to the organization which may then be publicised outside the organization. Sometimes, this may be for deliberate reasons.

A general example of the principle occurred in early 1990, when the French mineral water firm Perrier announced benzene contamination problems with their product. Although the nature of the announcement resulted in a clear loss of sales and market share the swift and thorough action taken by them may have helped retain customer confidence in the overall quality of the firm and its product.

In most cases, however, external publicity will be the result of a 'leak' of some kind. Media publicity can go beyond simple external publicity to address security weaknesses in a more generalised manner. As a simple example, specialist journals may print in-depth articles or reports on a particular threat to computer systems, possibly drawing on sample case studies, but not necessarily focusing on one organization.

For the organization itself, external publicity can be extremely problematic and, if uncontrolled, has the potential to be more serious than the security breakdown that provoked the coverage in the first place. Organizations may be reluctant to admit to problems for fear of questions about the competence of managers or directors. The dangers of publicity are easy to imagine.

For example, in July 1991 the newspaper *Computing* printed several articles reporting that the managing director of Data General in the United Kingdom had been obliged to write to customers following an internal security investigation, which had revealed that staff had been leaking company secrets to competitors, with resulting detrimental effects on the organization's ability to invest in, and deliver, the products and services that customers required.

Another more general example from 1989 concerns a confidential telephone hotline which was set up to collate material evidence for preliminary work on computer hacking legislation. At first, few calls were received, although the rate did eventually increase. The reason for the initial poor response was as a result of callers having to seek high-level permission before they could disclose the problems they had encountered. In many cases, the callers were terrified of adverse publicity.

However, if the media coverage can be made suitably anonymous, then the reaction of an organization to publicity of its problems is more likely to be positive. Research carried out by the author in 1991 to study organizational perception of security issues found that *generalised* media publicity of computer security issues was considered by organizations to be more of a benefit than a hindrance. Indeed, organizations recognised that such publicity could even be of benefit to them in two possible ways.

Firstly, it had the advantage of increasing the awareness of computer security threats, not just among the technical staff and policy-makers who had to deal with the threats, but also among ordinary staff such as secretaries and non-computing personnel. The fact that the awareness came from a source outside the organization meant that it was not so likely to be so casually discarded.

Secondly, media publicity of threats helped the developers of computer security policy by increasing *their* awareness of new and otherwise unknown threats. Some organizations might be worried that publicity could encourage computer attackers to explore using new methods that they might not otherwise have known about. However, in the worst case the organization as the defender would be in at least an equal position to learn about the risks at the same time as, or even before, the attackers.

Taking this observation to its conclusion, organizations may benefit from a central source of information dissemination which would provide warning of new threat sources. However, this will only work if organizations can have absolute confidence in the integrity, impartiality and security of the central source itself, qualities which are hard to achieve.

In practice, few organizations have any control over the way in which their difficulties can be represented by the media. The individual viewpoints of journalists, and the publications they write for, will inevitably influence the material and its presentation. As an example, one senior editor on a major British computer publication told the author that he was unwilling to approve stories on computer security breakdowns for fear of promoting 'copycat actions' elsewhere. Only if some aspect of the news item was significantly different from previous cases would he consider relaxing the rule.

CITY COMPUTER BLACKMAIL PLOT

by Gervase Webb

A BIZARRE blackmail plot to paralyse the City of London with a pernicious computer virus was being investigated by police today.

All over the Square Mile today staff in banks and other financial institutions received a personally addressed

'Pay $378' demand on Aids advice disks

woman said: "We have every reason to believe that there are a number of these disks in circulation."

She added: "They have been found to contain a virus

stop functioning normally." The Stock Exchange was guarded over the attempted sabotage. A spokesman said: "We have received a number of these disks, as have a number of other institutions in the City. We don't think it is part of a plot aimed specifically at the Stock Exchange, but we have taken it seriously enough to call in the police."

Police in the City said: "The envelopes are five and a

Figure 6: Headline from London *Evening Standard* newspaper, 13 December 1989

Although his approach was perhaps an extreme case, elements of such a philosophy appear to have wide acceptance. With the occasional exception of strange or unusual cases, which may form the headlines of newspapers (figure 6) and television news, it seems that computer security items are now relegated, in most instances, to the lesser importance of the inner pages of the computing press.

So how much does publicity really affect organizations? In general terms, it is frequently true that adverse publicity can have a significant effect upon the success of an organization, particularly in the short term. The severity of the effect will reflect any extenuating circumstances.

For example, a major fire on Tuesday 6th March 1990 at the customer services head office of Digital Equipment Corporation UK in Basingstoke had the potential to affect significantly the short term activities of the organization. However, within two days of the fire all the systems, networks and staff were back at work.

The ability of DEC to recover, thanks not least to its disaster recovery mechanisms, resulted in considerable interest from all sorts of people about disaster recovery procedures in practice. This meant that DEC was able to turn aspects of the misfortune to good effect, and build on its now tried and tested expertise in recovery to offer related services and advice to others.

The fact is that problems *do* occur in all organizations, and confidence in a business may be jeopardised far more by a failure to take adequate precautions than by the actual occurrence of an event.

Taking responsibility for spreading the message

Almost all organizations will have an inherent degree of security awareness from the perspective of preventing theft, vandalism and so on. Simple measures such as fitting locks to doors and windows, having alarms and lighting systems, and routine checks by security guards are well understood. In many cases, responsibilities of this kind form part of the domain of a buildings or facilities department. But the responsibility for computer security may not be so straightforward.

Typically, there are two departments, in particular, that play leading roles in the process of communicating security principles. These are the computer services and the personnel departments.

Members of computer services departments are likely to have a great deal of contact with technology and information systems users. In the course of their duties, such as installing or maintaining hardware and software, they will be coming into direct contact with the users, and are, therefore, provided with an ideal opportunity to observe if computer security policies are being followed.

This does not mean that computer services staff are necessarily taking on some form of secret policing role, but simply that they should, as a matter of course, check and verify a number of points as part of the normal service procedures.

For example, checks could be made that system access passwords have not been taped to the side of monitors, or that passwords have been changed recently. More usefully, a check could be made of what software has been installed, and whether it has been licensed. This check is also of relevance for technical reasons, as many problems can arise from unexpected interactions between certain combinations of software.

Computer services departments will certainly have a very good understanding of the technical side of computer security threats, not least because, following failures in systems, it will be part of their job to tidy up. However, they will be less interested in the personal or social aspects of the users that they deal with. This is viewed as being the responsibility of the personnel department.

A major objective of personnel departments is to know people. They have to be able to understand a variety of social and personal issues in order to be of help in addressing difficulties that individuals experience from time to time. How this is achieved depends in one respect upon the type of organization. For small organizations, personnel departments will largely handle the administration of employee details. For larger organizations, personnel staff may assist managers in improving the motivation, performance and satisfaction of employees.

Increasingly, personnel departments will have to address the issue of evaluating the responsibility and honesty of employees. Measures must be established for determining how well the individual works when subject to rules and regulations.

This does not mean that staff will be coerced or controlled in a forceful manner, but rather that employees should be able to understand why the rules and policies are necessary and actually contribute to the success and satisfaction of the tasks at hand.

This form of evaluation already occurs in employee appointment and review processes, particularly where financial functions are concerned. Someone will have the responsibility of deciding whether an employee can authorize payments up to $1,000, or $10,000, or $100,000, without referral to a higher authority. Clearly this represents a level of trust that the organization can recognise in financial terms. An equivalent measure is required for the organization to identify the security awareness and compliance, and hence trust, that an individual possesses.

So far as the security of computer-based information systems is concerned, there is a need for much greater liaison between the personnel, computer services, and the functional departments. Potential problems may be detected and corrected much earlier by generalised and on-going monitoring from all three perspectives. Reviews must be carried out diligently and thoroughly.

It may be very tempting to dismiss such reviews as being time-wasting and unproductive, especially if there is regular contact between the reviewer and reviewee. Unfortunately, in many organizations, the review process is performed by the reviewee's immediate superior as part of simple progress monitoring. This can result in much less thorough reviews, which in turn cause potential difficulties to be missed until they are much more significant and so become less easy to address and correct.

However, computer security issues cannot simply be appended to existing duties for either computer services or the personnel department. Unfortunately, this technique is often found in organizations where the presence of a department or team of specialists is seen as a suitable starting point, and effectively a dumping ground for the problem.

The apparent cost-effectiveness of this action in the short term may be considered sufficient justification for extending a departmental remit to include computer security responsibilities, rather than working hard to develop a new and wide-ranging approach to the issues.

Such a simplistic approach is highly unlikely to succeed. If responsibility is specifically allocated to an existing function, it is quite likely that the problems will not be analyzed sufficiently, or addressed comprehensively, because of the temptation to shape the responsibility according to the nature of the existing function. Furthermore, it is also possible that the original responsibilities of the department will suffer as a consequence of the added burden.

An alternative is to use a dedicated team of specialists for dealing with computer security. But this may allow some abdication of responsibility by other staff. If at any time an employee can defer responsibility to someone else, then the obligation to uphold that responsibility may be seen to have a lower priority, so as far as that employee is concerned, simply because 'it's not my responsibility'.

Finally, a dedicated team that focused upon computer security would soon come to represent a powerful 'force' within the organization. Reflecting the nature of the computer systems themselves, the team would have to cross all organizational boundaries and deal with all levels of management and staff. Of course, such a powerful and independent internal team is not likely to be popular in other departments.

Thus, it does not make sense to allocate the responsibility for spreading the message of computer security to a single team. Instead, it should be part of the duty and even contractual obligation of everyone who has anything to do with the organization's information systems. No one can be excluded from the duty of ensuring that security measures are understood and complied with at all times and by all people.

Dealing with transgressions

There is always the possibility that despite the publicity and enforcement of policies and procedures - and not just those relating to computer or information system security - some transgressions will occur. The matter then arises of how to treat these.

There may be national or local legislation in place which requires the organization to report the matter to the police for formal proceedings to take place. While these obligations must be fulfilled, it is easy to recognise that the organization may be reluctant to take action that may result in the kind of adverse publicity referred to earlier.

It should be noted, however, that for many cases of computer-related security breakdown, there will not be any point of specific interest and the case may not be reported at all in the media. As the number of occurrences of computer crime increase, so the appeal of each case to reporters declines.

Turning to internal action, there are two options open to the organization, depending upon the circumstances. The first is punishment reflecting the seriousness of the transgression. For most problems in an organization, it is a reasonably straightforward task to evaluate the severity of punishment required, and indeed standard disciplinary and appeal procedures will be part of the policy of the organization.

The difficulty when dealing with computer security transgression is that evaluation of the misconduct may be obscured by the complexity of the systems themselves.

For example, someone may have been copying confidential information, but it may not be so easy to determine what happened to that information afterwards. Accordingly, where computer security is concerned, the second option for dealing with transgressions may be applied.

The second option is instant dismissal, used for serious cases, and those cases where it is too dangerous to allow the employee a second chance. The employee shown to be responsible for the security breakdown is dismissed without being given an opportunity to inflict further damage. Suspects should be given every chance to defend themselves, but equally they should not be left unsupervised at any time until their innocence is assured.

If they have carried out a serious transgression of computer security policy, and dismissal is deemed appropriate, then full and effective removal from the premises is required. This may mean taking a variety of actions, including, as a minimum, the following:

- The offender cannot be allowed to return to their desk or office. Personal effects should be removed by other employees.
- The offender should certainly be barred from any access to organizational computer equipment.
- All passwords associated with systems to which the employee originally had access should be changed.
- All staff at all levels must be advised that the person is no longer employed by the organization.

A number of other steps may be taken according to circumstances, but the objective should always be to ensure that the offender does not get an opportunity to repeat or extend the damage that he or she caused. This applies both in the period during and immediately after disciplinary action is taken, and also for an extended subsequent time period. Many of these actions are, of course, applicable to other transgressions, and so are not specific to computer-related offenses. Indeed, in the majority of cases, the fact that an offence involved a computer system in some way may be almost totally irrelevant.

Each situation will be handled differently, according to organizational philosophy and the circumstances of the offence. It must be remembered, however, that the way in which computer security breakdowns are dealt with by the organization is in itself a means of spreading the message of security.

Any imagined or actual tolerance of an offender's actions can only serve to undermine the seriousness with which security policies are viewed and applied by other staff. Similarly, when taking steps to deal with the proven offender, it is unwise to understate the severity of the punishment. Regrettably, there are few cases where an *effective* example can be made by showing leniency.

Summary

In this chapter, we have looked at some of the problems of communicating the message of computer security. Unlike many other organizational issues, computer systems and information systems have an increasingly deep-rooted status. Failures in the systems can rapidly and dramatically affect the performance and success of the organization.

Accordingly, the systems must be protected, not only by the wealth of technological methods, but also by the awareness and cooperation of all staff in the organization. This in turn can best be achieved by greater publicity using methods that reflect the seriousness and unusual nature of the threats faced.

The boundaries of acceptable and unacceptable actions must be clear to all, along with the knowledge that transgression of the boundaries cannot be tolerated or excused.

6 Legislation

Important: this chapter is designed to provide a summary of some aspects of the subject matter covered. It does not purport to be comprehensive or to render legal advice.

- The concept of computer crime
- The need for privacy
- Data protection legislation
- System piracy, software copyright
- Computer misuse
- Summary

The matter of legislation is an important consideration in any discussion of security issues. In this chapter, we look at some aspects of legislation which relate to computer systems and computer security. It should be noted that it is impossible to provide comprehensive coverage of the subject, and obviously legislation varies from nation to nation. Therefore, a number of more general topics have been chosen as relevant and interesting examples.

Most countries perceive a need for some sort of legislation concerning computer systems and related aspects, but there are many variations in the actual implementation of the principles. It is even possible to construct an argument which questions the need for any computer-specific legislation at all, particularly if existing laws already appear to address the major issues.

The concept of computer crime

A good starting point is for us to consider what is meant by 'computer crime'. Although various instances of threats or attacks against computers might be referred to as computer crime, it is difficult to be really precise about *what* computer crime is. Despite the seemingly intuitive interpretation of the phrase, more careful consideration suggests that the concept is not clear at all, because there are a variety of very different activities that might all be referred to as computer crime.

For example, by the phrase computer crime, do we mean that a computer has somehow gained sentient awareness and proceeds to use its 'intelligence' in planning a criminal act? Or does computer crime mean that a computer system

110

was used by humans in preparing a largely non-technical crime such as a bank raid? Perhaps the crime was that a computer or software was actually stolen or damaged, or that a computer was used to 'hack into a bank'. Each of these interpretations *could* be taken as referring to computer crime, but in fact different laws would be used to deal with them.

Returning to what may loosely be termed the 'intuitive' understanding of computer crime, this perhaps refers to situations where one or more individuals have identified a weakness in a computer system, or recognised an alternative way in which it might be used. The computer criminals then exploit this new or alternative method for their own personal gain. This gain may be through monetary advantage, or it may be from malicious or intellectual satisfaction. So a 'computer crime' might be taken as meaning that the computer has been used simply as a tool to perform a criminal act.

If a prosecution is to brought against someone using non-computer-specific legislation, for example by application of an act of law concerning theft, then a number of factors may be required to indicate when a offence, thought to be a computer crime, has been committed.

Knowledge This factor requires that the person committing the crime is aware of what he or she is doing.

Purpose This factor requires that the person committing the crime must be shown to have had deliberate or reckless intent in performing the action.

Dishonesty This factor is required if the crime involves theft.

However, if computer-specific legislation is applied, new types of computer-specific crime may be defined which do not necessarily require all of the above factors to be present. For example, ignorance of the UK Data Protection Act does not provide an excuse for failure to register uses of personal data which are subject to the Act. This furthermore provides us with a fourth interpretation of 'computer crime', which describes offenses against computer-specific legislation.

Computer errors

The phrase computer crime is not the only one where ambiguities of meaning can arise. The claim of 'computer error' is often given as the reason for computer breakdowns. Yet in reality, it is extremely misleading for an organization to blame poor performance, careless service or accuracy problems of some kind on 'computer error'. Any organization which attempts to do so clearly does not appreciate the nature of computer technology, and this does not reflect well on their implementation of a computer-based information system.

The nature of current computer technology is such that, with very few exceptions, any form of genuine *computer* error would rapidly result in the system coming to a complete - and perhaps dramatic - halt. By contrast, errors in the processing of data, or in the display of results on a screen or the printed page, are unlikely to be due to the machine going wrong. Instead they will almost certainly be due to one of three basic causes:

* Incorrect design on the part of the system developers.
* Incorrect development where the design was not implemented correctly.
* Incorrect operation of the system itself, perhaps by operators, but most likely from poorly trained or careless users.

Any one of these three causes, and the last in particular, leads to situations where problems can occur that should be attributed to the human staff, not the computer system.

Interpretations

The two examples of 'computer crime' and 'computer error' illustrate that although phrases may be intuitively obvious, there may be a variety of possible interpretations that can be applied. This is relevant when the need arises for legal precedents to be established.

Most legislation is dependent upon the use of test-cases to identify the practical characteristics and nature of a new or untested law. Interpretation of legislation in a court is the only way to establish what a law means. However, interpretation may not be a straightforward task. In the two examples above, we have shown how easy it is for an ordinary person to recognise distinct variations in the interpretation of the phrase. It is likely that a legal expert would be able to establish a large number of possible meanings and interpretations for terms, any one of which might influence the subsequent effectiveness of a piece of legislation.

Our discussions need not be limited to computer crime or computer errors. For example, we could also address computer fraud, computer sabotage, and so on. All of these are related but distinct threats to computer systems and information systems. All contribute to the dilemma of defining clearly and formally the topic under consideration.

The conclusion is that when legal interpretation must be applied to information technology, the results are by no means clear-cut. Yet organizations must still have an appreciation of the law because they will be required to comply fully. Failure to observe laws may result in the organization and its representatives, the managers and board members being prosecuted.

The need for privacy

Laws provide a variety of means for dealing with theft, or violence, or various other problems that society faces, and of course an organization can call upon the law to help protect its property from such threats. But other items of legislation may apply not so much to the organization, but rather to those people and systems upon which the organization is based.

One of the most important applications of legislation to computer systems is to provide privacy, or protection of personal information from public knowledge. This is particularly important when computer systems are used, because technology makes it possible to process large quantities of personal data very rapidly. Cross-references and inferences may also be made using a process called data-matching. Here, unique identifiers such as names or addresses are used to match up personal information from different databases. Finally, computers can share and exchange this information in a manner which may be difficult to control.

One example of the problems concerns the provision of electronic mail or 'email' across computer networks. Some users make no attempt to use email, perhaps because it is perceived as being of no benefit to their work. Other people may vehemently refuse to use email because they consider it to be counter-productive. This view is based on the fact that vast numbers of messages can be received by some email users each and every day.

Nevertheless, the computerised nature of email is conducive to the formation of newsletters and special interest groups. The number of messages arriving each day from some of these news groups can certainly be measured in the hundreds.

The result could be that a user might have to spend several hours a day going through all the messages that have arrived from various sources, which is extremely time-consuming. Furthermore, many of the messages are of minimal value, being comments on previous messages, or comments on comments, and so on. Even those messages which *do* contain useful information are not easily distinguished from the other 'junk mail' messages.

Conversely, the use of email as a global discussion forum for interactive work can have outstanding benefits, as highlighted by several events in 1990 and 1991 involving the multi-national Internet. Notable examples include the post-event dissection of the Internet Worm to study how it worked and how similar threats could be stopped in the future; and the work by international physicists studying and attempting to duplicate the claim that cold-fusion reactions had been created in a test-tube. Another interesting example was the use of a real-time 'chat' system that enabled users to 'listen' as other users all over the world made comments and discussed events during the Gulf War. Sometimes there would be brief pauses as people in the region had to put on their gas masks.

However, the provision of electronic mail also brings issues of personal privacy into question. If messages are being transmitted by computer, it is technically possible for the owners or operators of the computer network to examine the contents of those messages. This exact problem has already been demonstrated in some US organizations. In 1990, Epson America was sued for monitoring staff email messages and for wrongful dismissal of a staff member after she complained about the eavesdropping.

In a similar case, Nissan Motor in the US was alleged to have monitored email messages between two information systems employees, who then proceeded with a lawsuit which accused Nissan of invasion of privacy, violations of constitutional right of privacy and wrongful termination of employment. The two ex-employees said that the company felt they were making excessive use of the system and monitored their messages. They then said they were rebuked for overusing the system, and when they complained about invasion of their privacy they were sacked.

It would appear that a simple prohibition of such monitoring might be sufficient to deal with the problem. However, the matter is complicated by the fact that in some areas, network operators may actually be *obliged* to monitor network traffic, simply in order to ensure free passage of information, or to prevent abuse of the network. Thus there is a need to resolve the clear conflict of interest between an individual's right to privacy, and the duties of the network operator.

Another example of information privacy might involve a mail order firm. Such an organization could be *functionally* unconcerned by possible inaccuracies in the names and addresses on its mailing list. A large proportion of its data will remain sufficiently accurate to be delivered to a particular household, in which case the objective of advertising will have been achieved. The number of mail shots which are 'lost' or cannot be delivered at all will be of an insignificant level.

However, this broad scale approach to advertising may be a problem if the recipient does not want to receive the advertisements. In an attempt to counteract the backlash of discontent, and avoid their promotional literature being discarded instantly, advertisers and other information providers have started to develop wide-ranging and comprehensive databases that record data about personal preferences and dislikes, and also information about demographic trends. This enables them to 'target' their advertising material towards people who are more likely to be interested in the products being offered.

For example, if you live in a comparatively wealthy neighborhood, you are also more likely to take foreign holidays, or have two cars, and a large garden, and so on. By contrast, a family living in a depressed area is not so likely to have a garden, they may have only one car, and so on. Distinctions such as these will be used to identify products or services that may be of interest or relevance to the recipient.

Every piece of data that can be collected about you represents more information for the database about you, your lifestyle, and your environment. This in turn enables advertisers, or indeed anyone else with access to the same information, to 'tailor' their work to reflect your individual characteristics.

It is not surprising that this kind of data collection is causing some concern, and not only among those who wish to protect their privacy. It may be that the collection of the data is for perfectly straightforward purposes, with no ulterior motive. However, once the information has been entered into a computer, it can be transmitted to other systems, cross-referenced, and generally processed in a manner totally different to the original purpose.

Thus, although the organization may have no operational reason for protecting data and limiting its use to certain, approved purposes, there may be a need for other obligations, perhaps imposed by social responsibility, or even legislation, to *force* the organization to take appropriate measures.

The need for privacy legislation concerning computer systems derives in the main from the technical facility to process lots of data quickly. Until the advent of the computer, it was possible for people to retain a considerable degree of privacy over their circumstances due to the fact that the paperwork and administration necessary to track even a single individual was considerable.

Today, several estimates suggest that in most advanced nations, personal information about *every* individual will be 'considered' or in some way 'processed' by a computer system, for some purpose, at least six times every day. In a true information society, such as that to which we are moving at an increasing rate, individuals will not be able to hide. Every use of a credit card, every telephone call made using a digital exchange, every use of a library represents another point at which information about your activities, your location, and your intentions could be collected. Far from allowing an individual to be lost among administrative bureaucracy, modern information systems can trace, process, and cross-reference details about you at the speed of light.

The issue of personal privacy in the electronic age must address the potential for not just one, but an entire globe, full of 'big brothers', processing and cross-referencing information far more quickly and impassionately than anything George Orwell ever envisaged.

The use of legislation for dealing with issues such as privacy is not straightforward. As an example, an American organization called the Electronic Frontier Foundation or EFF was formed in 1990 by a group of people including computer industry pioneers Steve Wozniak and Mitch Kapor, who were respectively cofounders of Apple and Lotus.

In 1991 the EFF funded an attack on the US Computer Fraud and Abuse Act of 1986, claiming that it was unconstitutional and prevented free speech. Lawyers representing the EFF said that the wording in the Act, which states that it is illegal to share information concerning 'any password or similar information through which a computer may be accessed without authorization', was too vague. Furthermore, it was suggested that the wording prevented specialists from discussing or working on computer security issues, and could in turn inhibit the development of better computer security measures.

Similar difficulties were identified in a proposed anti-terrorism law in the US to limit the sale of products designed to make computer systems secure, and which could actually lead to an increase in computer crime. Senate bill 266, which was known as the Comprehensive Anti-terrorism Act of 1991, sought to prevent terrorists from using technology that could protect them from eaves-dropping by authorities. The problem was that this same technology could also be used by businesses to secure data communications and so help protect systems from unauthorized access.

The bill stated that 'providers of electronic communications services and manufacturers of electronic communications service equipment shall ensure that communications systems permit the government to obtain the plain text contents of voice, data, and other communications when appropriately authorized by law.' In order to comply with the anti-terrorist act, security firms would have to keep copies of access keys used by customers, so that government agencies could monitor computer exchanges. The effect would be that firms would try to sell secure systems but at the same time would have to admit that the systems were not proof against government eavesdropping.

Thus it is rarely a simple matter to identify a problem which has been created by information technology, and then to proceed to develop legislation to counter those same problems.

Data protection legislation
Most advanced nations have some form of legislation which addresses the privacy of computerised data. The European nations in particular have an interesting situation. The European Commission has a long history of

involvement and interest in data protection issues, and as early as 1975 the European Parliament instructed the Commission to consider the production of a directive to deal with the problem of implementing suitable and internationally recognised legislation.

In a separate development in October 1980, the Organization for Economic Co-operation and Development (OECD) produced a recommendation concerning guidelines governing the protection of privacy, and transborder flows of personal data. Eighteen of the twenty-four member nations of the OECD adopted the recommendation. The UK was one of the six countries to abstain.

Several nations took action early on to address the privacy of computerised data. However, the efforts of many European nations were intended primarily to comply with the 1981 Council of Europe Convention on Data Protection (see table 8), to which the UK was one of eleven signatories.

The convention came into force on 1st October 1985, but by mid-1991 only seven community states had ratified the convention. This meant that data users in the community were still operating under significantly different conditions, which in turn meant that barriers could be placed in the way of transborder data flows. The effect upon organizations was that they might not be free to import or export operational data.

Following criticisms made in 1989 by data protection commissioners from the community nations, and in view of the imminent European free market from 1st January 1993, the European Commission made a renewed effort to develop a common approach to the issues. The problem was that one of the objectives of the internal European market is to support the free exchange of information using transborder data transmission, with a view to aiding work in such fields as the environment, health care and social services. One of the most ironic aspects was that the personal information databases of the Commission's own institutions were not subject to data protection legislation. There was a need for a complete and consistent approach to the implementation of basic principles of data protection throughout the community nations, and affecting all community activities.

Unless these issues were addressed, there was a real possibility that members of the community could restrict transborder dataflow, erect obstacles to economic activity, distort competition, and even obstruct the Commission's supervisory functions. Therefore, there was a need for all member states to have equivalent levels of protection of privacy in relation to the computer-processing of data.

Table 8: Summary of key articles in 1981 Council of Europe Convention on data protection

---

Article 3: Scope
The Convention applies to all public and privately owned automated personal data files and may be extended by any State to manual files

---

Article 5: Quality of data
Personal data shall be:
- Obtained and processed fairly and lawfully
- Stored for specified and legitimate purposes and not used in a way incompatible with those purposes.
- Adequate, relevant and not excessive in relation to the purposes for which they are stored.
- Accurate and, where necessary, kept up-to-date.
- Preserved in a form which permits identification of the Data Subjects for no longer than is required for the purposes for which these data are stored.

Article 6: Special categories of data
Personal data revealing racial origin, political opinions, religious or other beliefs, health or sexual life, as well as personal data relating to criminal convictions, may not be processed automatically unless domestic law provides appropriate safeguards

---

Article 7: Data security
Appropriate security measures for personal data shall be taken against accidental or unauthorised destruction or accidental loss as well as against unauthorised access, alteration or dissemination

---

Article 8: Additional safeguards for the Data Subject
Any person has a right to:
- Establish the existence of an automated personal data file, its main purposes, and the name and address of the controller of the file.
- Know whether a data file has information relating to that person and obtain the contents of that information at reasonable intervals and without excessive delay or expense.
- Obtain the rectification or erasure of such data if these have been processed contrary to a basic set of data protection principles.

Article 9: Exceptions and restrictions
Exceptions from the provisions listed above are allowed in order to:
- Protect public safety, State security or monetary interests of the State, or the suppression of criminal offenses.
- Protect the Data Subject or the rights and freedoms of others.

Suggested revisions to the European Convention

By June 1991, the Commission had put forward a proposal for a revised general directive to the European Council of Ministers, with the intention that it should be binding on member states by 1st January, 1993.

The key statements in the draft directive extended the terms of the earlier Convention in a number of ways:

- 'Private sector organizations will be obliged to inform the data subject when their data is first made available for online access.'
- 'The controller of the file shall take appropriate technical and organizational measures to protect personal data ... against accidental or unauthorized destruction or loss or unauthorized access, modification or processing.'
- 'Individuals from whom personal data have been collected have the right to be informed ... about the purposes of the file for which the information is intended.'
- 'No individual is to be subject to an administrative or private decision involving an assessment of his conduct which has as its sole basis the automatic processing of personal data.'
- 'The individual will have the right to oppose for legitimate reasons the processing of personal data relating to him.'
- 'Methods guaranteeing adequate security shall be chosen for the transmission of personal data in a network.'

However, there were two further requirements which had extremely significant implications:

- 'The definitions are extended to include structured automated and manual files.'
- 'Any copies of data previously passed to third parties must also be corrected.'

The draft directive was immediately criticised for a number of reasons. Many aspects were thought to go to far, to be too bureaucratic, and impossible within the chosen timescale. By including manual data such as paperwork into the draft directive, procedures for providing data protection would be made significantly more complicated.

Commentators were quick to point out that this would have considerable and worrying implications for any organization wishing to use computers or indeed manual systems for processing personal information.

For the present, the details of the draft directive will continue to be the subject of much manoeuvring, with both industry representatives and governments trying to make changes to suit their particular viewpoints. It is possible that by publishing the highest possible data protection standards, the Commission has deliberately provoked widescale discussions, and perhaps expects to give ground in some areas. Whatever the outcome, the final directive will be of significant importance to both the data users and those about whom data is collected.

The UK Data Protection Act 1984

As one of the signatories to the 1981 Convention, the UK had to develop national legislation to implement its principles. The Convention had twenty Articles, the most significant of which have been summarised in table 8. In conjunction with these and earlier government work, a White Paper was issued in April 1982 outlining the general principles of the proposed UK data protection legislation. A Data Protection Bill finally received Royal Assent, becoming law on 12 July 1984.

The Data Protection Act 1984 has five Parts, each with a specific purpose. Part I sets out the definitions and principles underlying the legislation. Part II defines the registration process. Part III defines the right of Data Subjects. Part IV defines the exemptions, and Part V provides rules for the duties and powers of the individual charged with maintaining the register (the Registrar), the role of public sector bodies, and the scope of the legislation. Part I of the Act sets out eight Data Protection Principles (see table 9), which are based upon the key principles of the 1981 European Convention.

In order to improve understanding, the Act goes to great lengths to define what is meant by 'Data', 'Personal Data', 'Data Subjects', and 'Data Users'. A brief summary of the definitions is given in table 10.

For some organizations, the Act may be viewed as an additional administrative burden with substantial penalties for non-compliance. However, the obligation to comply with the Act can be viewed as an excellent opportunity to review existing or planned data processing facilities. Any organization which fails to register, and which is not exempt from the Act, would be committing an offence, regardless of the reason for non-registration. Similarly, failing to keep a registration up-to-date is also a criminal offence, as is knowingly or recklessly using, obtaining, disclosing or transferring (including to another country) personal data other than as described in the registration entry.

In particular there are several issues that must be addressed by all organizations to some extent, and which are outlined here.

Table 9: The Principles of the UK Data Protection Act 1984

The First Principle
The information to be contained in personal data shall be obtained, and personal data processed, fairly and lawfully.

The Second Principle
Personal data shall be held only for one or more specified and lawful purposes.

The Third Principle
Personal data held for any purpose or purposes shall not be used or disclosed in any manner incompatible with that purpose or purposes.

The Fourth Principle
Personal data held for any purposes shall be adequate, relevant and not excessive in relation to that purpose or purposes.

The Fifth Principle
Personal data shall be accurate and, where necessary, kept up-to-date.

The Sixth Principle
Personal data held for any purpose or purposes shall not be kept for longer than is necessary for that purpose or those purposes.

The Seventh Principle
An individual shall be entitled:
(a)   at reasonable intervals and without delay or expense:
    (i)   to be informed by any data user whether he holds personal data of which that individual is the subject; and
    (ii) to access to any such data held by a data user; and
(b)   where appropriate, to have such data corrected or erased.

The Eighth Principle
Appropriate security measures shall be taken against unauthorised access to, or alteration, disclosure or destruction of, personal data and against accidental loss or destruction of personal data.

Table 10: Summary of key definitions in UK Data Protection Act 1984.

Term	Interpretation
Data	Data means information recorded in a form in which it can be processed automatically in response to instructions given for that purpose.
Personal Data	Personal Data means Data consisting of information which relates to a living individual who can be identified from that information (or from that and other information in the possession of the Data User), including any expression of opinion of the intentions of the Data User in respect of that individual.
Data Subject	Data Subject means an individual who is the subject of Personal Data.
Data User	Data User means a person who holds Data, and a person 'holds' Data if: (a) The Data form part of a collection of Data processed or intended to be processed by or on behalf of that person; and (b) That person (either alone or jointly or in common with other persons) controls the contents and use of the Data comprised in the collection; and (c) The Data are in a form in which they have been or are intended to be processed as mentioned in (a) above or (though not for the time being in that form) in a form into which they have been converted after being so processed and with a view to being further so processed on a subsequent occasion.

Compliance policy Someone within the organization, perhaps a Data Protection Officer, must take the responsibility for looking after the organization's observation of the Act. This will require knowledge of computer systems, the organization, and the Act itself.

Registration and maintenance All relevant data material held or processed by the organization must be identified. This will include material processed locally and remotely, on centralised machines and distributed small computers.

The process of registration is on-going in the sense that all the details must be kept up-to-date. Each registration lasts for a period of three years, at which point a renewal procedure must be applied. Additionally, the Data Protection Officer or colleagues must review the organization at frequent intervals.

This is to ensure continuing compliance with the principles of the Act, that the material being processed by the computer systems is still compatible with the current registration, and that staff are aware of their responsibilities.

Inspection by subjects The Act gives people, or Data Subjects, the right to access data about themselves. The user of an information system, the Data User, must therefore make provision for such access. It is particularly important that the access procedure should include identification checking mechanisms to prevent the possibility of wrongful disclosure.

Changes to data It is possible that after a Data Subject has seen the information held by the Data User, corrections may be considered necessary because of inaccuracies. Modifications or even erasure of the data may be required by order of a court or the Data Protection Registrar.

In July 1989, the Data Protection Registrar presented a report to the UK Parliament which included a review of the working of the Act since it took full effect in November 1987. In the report, the Registrar made a number of recommendations for changes to the Data Protection Act, which included a simpler registration process, a clarification of the meaning of the Act, and simplification of the way in which the Act is applied to make it more effective.

However, before discussion of these recommendations could make any great progress, the European Commission issued its draft proposal for revised data protection legislation. In July 1991 the Registrar acknowledged that the 1989 recommendations would 'have to take a back seat while consideration of the draft directive takes place.' There is little doubt that the new directive from the European Commission, when it appears, will have a radical effect upon the UK Data Protection Act.

The future for data protection

The European single market that will exist after 1992 will certainly result in much larger quantities of personal data being transmitted across borders. However, the effects of data protection legislation in a transborder environment is not restricted to the European Community.

Not least, many US companies will in future have to consider the implication of European laws upon their trading activities. Many US businesses are used to comparatively few restrictions upon usage of data on employees and customers.

But movement of data to or from European nations may be constrained by the fact that companies will have to inform every person in a particular database if they plan to use the database for any other purpose. In particular, Article 24 of the Commission's directive on Data Protection is intended to stop the export of personal data to countries lacking adequate data protection laws, although the meaning of 'adequate' is not defined. There is a strong possibility that US companies may face the prospect of stricter data privacy laws at home, not only to facilitate transborder information exchange, but also to recognise growing discontent from within the US itself.

While businesses may be worried at the prospect of restrictions on the previously unregulated exchange of personal information in computerised databases, others may welcome the right to check accuracy of information and to have some control over how that information is being used.

A graphic example of this was provided in January 1991, when Lotus Development Corporation was obliged to abandon a CD-ROM based direct marketing system, called Marketplace Households. The planned database, holding personal information on more than 120 million US citizens and 80 million households, was abandoned after more than 30,000 people protested to Lotus in a two-week period, all concerned about the inclusion of their details in the database.

Lack of control over personal data means that victims may be unable to obtain credit or even jobs because of inaccuracies in the data. Fortune 500 corporations regularly check on their staff, taking advantage of access to databases. Complaints from US residents about how databases of personal information are collected, coupled with the need to harmonise legislation to permit transborder data flow, may mean that the European model for data protection may influence future US laws in this area.

System piracy, software copyright

One of the biggest problems for system developers is piracy of their products. As an example, research suggests that in the UK, only 83 software packages are sold for every 100 personal computers. A survey carried out by the Software Publishers Association and the Business Software Alliance found that Italy has a particularly bad problem with only 0.55 software packages per PC in 1990. This actually represents an improvement since 1988, when the figure was 0.17 packages. In Europe as a whole, software piracy costs the IT industry around $4.5 billion in lost revenue (see figure 7).

Strictly speaking, there is a distinction between software piracy and software copying. Piracy, which may be a criminal act depending on the country in which it occurs, is where illicit copies of programs are sold, offered for hire, or imported. By contrast, copying is often a civil offence, and is carried out mainly by employees making 'backup' copies for themselves or friends.

The problem is that copying software is generally very easy to do, particularly in the case of personal computers. Here, the necessity for standardization means that software cannot be protected against copying by employing

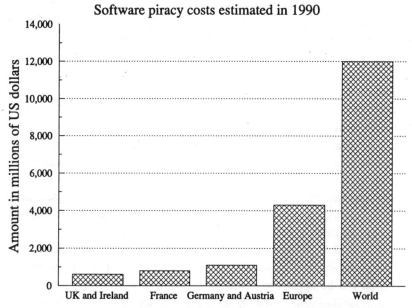

Figure 7: Software piracy costs

unique characteristics of the computer system itself. The nearest approximation is to use a hardware device called a 'dongle', which plugs into one of the ports that all personal computers have. Software packages can then check to see if the dongle is present.

The problem is that dongles are perceived as being likely to interfere with the operation of other software, and even come into conflict with other dongle-based packages, although there appears to be no documented cases of such problems. Despite their effectiveness, therefore, dongles are not a popular method of protecting software.

The difficulty for software developers is that there are some circumstances when it is desirable that users *should* copy software, mainly for sensible reasons such as backing-up packages to protect their investment. Accordingly, some programs have a mechanism built-in that requires the user to enter an identification label before the package can be installed for the first time.

This has the advantage that licensed backups of software are allowed, and that each copy or backup can be associated with its original owner. However, the experienced user quickly recognises this sort of mechanism, and can bypass it by copying disks using a 'bit-copier' package *before* the identification tag is put onto the master disk.

A final method is to code each copy of the software uniquely before it is sent out to users. Unfortunately, this does not *prevent* the owner from making multiple copies. But another major disadvantage of this technique is that it prevents the developer from using a mass-duplication system themselves, because each copy must be unique and then associated with the eventual owner.

As to the question of *why* software is copied, the most common reason given when offenders are questioned seems to be based upon the assumption that 'it doesn't do anyone any harm'. While it might appear that copying of software saves the organization some money in the short-term, it is not true in the longer term.

Quite apart from the existence of legislation that makes software copying a criminal offence, illegal copying of software constrains investment in the software development industry. This means that development costs are pushed up, and consequently end-user purchase costs are increased. It is interesting to note that countries with no protection for software developers have almost no indigenous software industry.

As with data privacy, most nations have some form of legislation that addresses copyright of materials and in most, but not all situations, this legislation can be applied to computer software as well. Some nations have corrected loopholes in existing laws by developing new legislation that specifically addresses the protection of computer programs. But, as with data protection, there are often dramatic differences in the laws between countries.

In an attempt to address some of these problems, the European Commission issued a draft directive on the subject on 5th January 1989. The intention of the Commission was that provision should be made for software to be protected under European law, but at the same time that the development of software should not be constrained.

Naturally, legislation in this area is of primary interest to systems development organizations, but it *also* has implications for end-user organizations which make use of computer systems.

For example, under the Commission proposal, the owner of the software copyright would be the author of the software, rather than the person or organization paying for it. This would mean that an organization which requires a specific system and commissions an external software house to develop the system, would not be the copyright owner. As a result, the software house would then be able to go out and sell the product to other organizations.

Perhaps the most contentious issue highlighted during the discussions over the directive concerned the concept of reverse engineering. This is a technique where a delivered program is carefully analyzed to determine the original program instructions, the 'source code', used to produce the program. This technique is often used by programmers to help them understand how other programs work.

Ideally, programmers would like the original program and its design principles to have been well documented, and this information placed into the public domain. However, for obvious commercial reasons, the practical reality is that, in most situations, information of this kind will not be widely available outside the original development organization.

A major example of this issue concerns the use of computer networks. Typically, a programmer wishes to develop a system that will successfully interface with the network. If insufficient documentation is available, the programmer may have no alternative but to examine existing functional programs to see how they work.

In particular, a major objective would be to determine how the systems might interconnect with other programs or systems. Such is the importance of this goal, also known as interoperability, that it became a major part of the debate over reverse engineering.

A number of European and Japanese hardware manufacturers, including Bull, Apricot, NCR, Olivetti and Fujitsu, joined together in a group called the European Committee for Interoperable Systems, or ECIS. They alleged that the draft directive on the legal protection of computer programs would harm the move to open systems by making interface software copyrightable, and in general making it much more difficult to develop compatible but competing products. By contrast, the Software Action Group for Europe, or SAGE, which was made up of some of the world's largest suppliers including IBM, DEC, Microsoft and Lotus, welcomed the Commission's directive as it seemed to suggest stronger protection for their products.

The European Commission was therefore attempting to address two conflicting issues.

Firstly, it was keen to promote the development of interoperable systems, and prior experience suggested that reverse engineering was almost a prerequisite for this to be possible.

Secondly, the directive did not directly address the issue of reverse engineering, and was therefore interpreted as meaning that reverse engineering was not allowed without permission from the copyright owner of the original software.

The draft proposal was submitted to the European Parliament for consideration in July 1990 and, in the light of the views offered by the Parliament, and the various representations made by both ECIS and SAGE, an amended proposal was issued in October 1990. Further debate ensued, resulting in the European Council approving the directive subject to a number of further amendments. The directive was finally adopted and formally published in May 1991.

The directive, now known as the European Software Directive, has a number of implications for user organizations. The holder of software program rights has the authority to reproduce, translate, adapt, arrange, alter and distribute the program. The holder is defined as being the author or authors that created the program. Consequently, all rights regarding the program will belong to the author rather than the contractor, unless otherwise acquired under contract.

Of particular interest to end-user organizations is Article 5.2 of the directive, which states that 'the making of a backup copy by a person having a right to use the computer program may not be prevented by contract insofar as it is necessary for that use.'

The goal of trying to achieve interoperable systems has also been addressed. Under the directive, users cannot be prevented from observing, studying and testing a program in order to discover its underlying ideas and principles, so long as those actions are within the boundaries of permitted use.

Going further, there are now conditions where reverse engineering is possible. If the necessary information is not readily available to a lawful user, then lawful users may decompile the program and so reverse engineer only the relevant parts of the program. The information obtained by reverse engineering under those conditions may *only* be used to achieve interoperability of independently created programs, and *cannot* be supplied to third parties (except where necessary to achieve interoperability), nor can it be used to develop a substantially similar program or for any other act which infringes copyright.

By taking into account all the various views from interested parties, the European Commission was able to issue a directive that met with approval from all parties involved. The directive does not hamper the movement toward truly open systems and ensures that developers continue to have the ability to create and sell original and competitive computer products.

Computer misuse

For most organizations, the most important legislation concerning computer security is likely to be those laws which deal with problems such as computer viruses, and in particular, hackers. Theoretically, many forms of computer security problems could be dealt with using existing legislation. Using a computer to commit a fraud is still a fraud. Damaging a computer or data using a computer virus is still criminal damage.

Dealing with hacking may be a little more difficult, and in one notorious case the British House of Lords ruled that two hackers, Stephen Gold and Robert Schifreen, could not be prosecuted under the Forgery and Counterfeiting Act of 1981, even though they had broken into the Duke of Edinburgh's private electronic mail system in 1985 using false identification passwords. Other attempts to prosecute hackers involved the use of the Theft Act 1978 for stealing electricity to run the computers.

In 1989, the British Law Commission started work on identifying suitable recommendations to deal with computer misuse. In October of that year, a report was published which suggested the creation of three criminal offenses to make hackers and virus writers accountable for their actions, whether performed in fun or for devious reasons.

Much of the work took into account experiences documented in the US, Canada, Sweden and France. At the time, most US states had passed laws on computer crime, and several had statutes that addressed the problem of computer viruses being inserted into systems.

In New York, a leading state in the field, it is an offence to gain unauthorized access to confidential information, or to inflict more than $1,000 of damage. In California, the State Assembly enhanced its existing computer crime laws by revising its definition of networks and banning academic institutions from awarding degrees related to computer sciences to anyone convicted of computer crimes.

Congress had passed its Computer Fraud and Abuse Act in 1984, and strengthened it further in 1986. This Act identified a number of criminal offenses, defined as an individual carrying out any one of the actions described in table 11. The Act carries penalties of up to five years in prison and $250,000 in fines.

The first successful prosecution under the Computer Fraud and Abuse Act came in January 1989, when 17-year-old Herbert Zinn from Chicago was arrested and sentenced to nine months in prison for hacking into the computers of the AT&T telephone company, NATO, and the Department of Defense. Zinn, or 'Shadowhawk' as he tagged himself, copied $1.2 million worth of programs and published top secret passwords on electronic bulletin boards in Chicago and Texas.

However, the emphasis on an individual having unauthorized access to a computer system means that the Act is not so suitable for dealing with the dramatic upsurge of problems caused by computer viruses. At the time that the Computer Fraud and Abuse Act was under consideration, computer viruses were an almost unknown concept.

In order to correct this weakness, two further Bills, the Computer Virus Eradication Bill and the Computer Protection Bill, are being presented to Congress. These will make it illegal for people to tamper with data held on computer, and will carry a prison sentence of up to 15 years. As an aside, it is interesting to note that the creator of the Internet Worm, Robert Morris, was successfully prosecuted under the Computer Fraud and Abuse Act.

Table 11: Criminal actions defined in US Computer Fraud and Abuse
Act 1986

{1030(a)(1)} 'knowingly ... obtains information that has been determined by the U.S. Government ... to require protection against unauthorised disclosure for reasons of national defense or foreign relations, ... or any restricted data as defined in ... the Atomic Energy Act of 1954';

{1030(a)(2)} 'intentionally ... obtains information contained in a financial record of a financial institution ... or contained in a file of a consumer reporting agency on a consumer, as such terms are defined in the Fair Credit Reporting Act ...';

{1030(a)(3)} '... intentionally accesses a computer without authorization if such computer is exclusively for the use of the Government of the United States or, in the case of a computer not exclusively for such use, if such computer is used by or for the Government of the United States and such conduct affects such use';

{1030(a)(4)} 'knowingly and with intent to defraud, accesses a Federal interest computer without authorization, or exceeds authorized access, and by means of such conduct furthers the intended fraud and obtains anything of value, unless the object of the fraud and the thing obtained consists only of the use of the computer';

{1030(a)(5)} 'intentionally accesses a Federal interest computer without authorization, and by means of one or more instances of such conduct alters information in that computer, or prevents authorized use of that computer, and thereby causes loss to one or more others of a value aggregating $1,000 or more during any one year period';

{1030(a)(6)} 'knowingly and with intent to defraud traffic (as defined in section 1029) in any passwords or similar information through which a computer may be accessed without authorization, if a) such trafficking affects interstate or foreign commerce; or b) such computer is used by or for the Government of the United States.'

The UK Computer Misuse Act 1990

In December 1989, a Conservative party MP, Michael Colvin, presented a Computer Misuse Bill for consideration by the House of Commons. The Bill drew heavily upon the earlier work of the Law Commission. Following approval by both the House of Commons and the House of Lords, the Bill received Royal Assent on 29th June 1990, and the new Computer Misuse Act 1990 came into force on 29 August 1990.

The Act introduced three new offences into English Law. The first, described under section One, is an offence of basic unauthorized access. The second, section Two, deals with unauthorized access with intent to facilitate the commission of more serious crime. The third, section Three, makes it an offence to cause unauthorized modification to the contents of any computer. The Act also clarifies the relevant parts of the earlier Criminal Damage Act 1971, to explain how it could apply to computer material, which is not necessarily 'tangible'.

The scope of section One of the Computer Misuse Act 1990 is deliberately very wide, as it enables the Act to apply to all kinds of unauthorized access, regardless of the motives of the hacker. The reference to more serious crime in section Two is to address the possible use of a computer in an offence such as theft or blackmail.

In effect, it is now possible to prosecute someone who inserts a logic bomb into a computer system and demands payment before it can be removed. Section Three deals with the possibility of data being corrupted, either directly by the offender, or indirectly following the actions of a virus or similar device constructed by the offender.

The jurisdiction of the Computer Misuse Act 1990 provides that prosecutions can be brought either when the offender is in the United Kingdom, or the computer that was accessed or modified is within the jurisdiction, or if any further offence (as covered by section Two) were to occur in the jurisdiction.

So far as most organizations are concerned, perhaps the most important feature of the Computer Misuse Act is the importance of authorization in accessing the computer or modifying material. For an offence to have been committed under the Act, the necessary access or modification must have been unauthorized.

For those security threats that arise from outside the organization, this is not much of a problem. However, given the large number of threats that are carried out by staff from within the organization, it is *essential* that levels of authority are clearly defined for each member of the organization, and that these levels are reviewed regularly. It would be a good idea to implement warning screens on all computer systems that indicate that certain levels of authority are required to proceed further, and that transgression represents unauthorized access.

Finally, for a successful prosecution to be possible under the Act, the victim organization must be able to provide evidence of the actions of the offender. This will include a list of dates and times when the events took place; a description of how system access control mechanisms had been bypassed, with a list of any relevant passwords and usernames; and a record of what actions where carried out by the offender once access had been gained.

Summary

In this chapter, we have considered some of the issues that apply when legislation is used to deal with computer security problems. One of the most important observations is that such legislation is very new and frequently untested. In practice, there are only three worthwhile ways of determining whether a particular piece of legislation has any real meaning.

The first is the successful prosecution of an offender who has not admitted guilt.

The second is determination of the limits of the legislation by identifying those cases which are not prosecuted under the legislation, because they were not considered part of the original objectives.

The third is by the collection of material evidence which shows the effectiveness of the legislation at deterring the specific criminal acts.

Prosecution of computer security offenders is still a comparatively unusual event, although in 1989 the US National Center for Computer Crime Data reported that the estimated number of prosecutions for computer crime had risen to 2,000, representing a ten-fold increase over a three-year period.

For all practical purposes, the best course of action for an organization to follow would be to take steps to ensure that security is not breached, and thus there is no need to recourse to prosecution under computer crime laws.

7 Where next for computer security?

- **The effectiveness of controls**
- **From computer security to systems integrity**
- **Summary**

In this chapter, we expand upon some of the key points made in previous chapters, and extend our discussion into a slightly more philosophical domain.

It is interesting to begin by noting that in practice, the typical American employee now works around 47 hours a week, on average. During the course of a full employment year, this represents an additional 164 hours of work than twenty years ago.

Undoubtedly, one of the major reasons for this extra worktime is technology, and in particular computer systems. Devices such as modems, laptop and portable computers, faxes and cellular phones have all started to demolish the boundaries of the workplace. The availability of cheap but powerful computers has meant that many commuters are able to take work home with them, and may even be able to work while travelling.

Increasingly, it is possible and even *expected* that employees should be productive and accessible at any hour of any day. A glance through reviews of portable computer technology quickly reveals the current preoccupation with providing a powerful system that can be used almost anywhere.

Indeed, for employers to provide this kind of portable technology to every member of staff could be considerably more cost-effective than paying the overtime that would otherwise be necessary. Several large organizations now provide computer equipment for home use on precisely this form of cost-justification.

Further evidence of the use of personal systems comes from the observation that implementation of computer technology is moving away from the earlier centralised system to become a more distributed resource. In simple data processing terms, a survey of 200 European users showed that currently, 43% of data is processed on mainframes, 29% on minicomputers, and 28% on desktop PCs. By 1993, the figures are predicted to change to 40% mainframe and 31% PC. In the UK, the figures are already measured as 35% mainframe and 30% PC. Inevitably, as work devolves more to an individual rather than group activity, so the nature of work itself changes.

These facts, combined with the once-laudable goals of computer literacy, have resulted in a significant portion of workers, at all levels in society, being well aware of how to use computer technology. However, in many cases they remain largely unaware of how technology can relate to real problems and, more importantly, how they themselves can handle real problems.

Few people could attempt the task of developing a word-processor or spreadsheet package, even after the successful completion of a university degree course. Yet this is apparently where the thrust of training appears to be directed, with minimal emphasis on understanding why we would want to perform a task, let alone what its implications will be for the employing organization.

But there is an alternative explanation that could be offered for our lack of understanding of the issues. This might be due to the fact that computers are a 'new technology'. If so, it would mean that we have not yet had the opportunity to understand fully their implications for user organizations. This would be exacerbated by the extremely rapid pace of technology development.

However, the reality is rather different. Computers are no longer a new technology, and there have already been substantial opportunities for organizations and individuals to recognise and address their implications. Sufficient expertise now exists such that where once it was a major task to program a computer to perform a simple addition, today we think nothing of performing what are truly astonishing tasks using incomprehensible quantities of information.

Furthermore, such power is no longer restricted to the supercomputer or super-expensive mainframes that could only be bought by large corporations. Today, for a modest outlay, anyone can purchase a desk-top machine that offers considerable processing resources. Such systems can now process small quantities of data in a very small amount of time, while large quantities can be processed in an acceptable time.

Early in the history of computing, it was estimated that at most six computers would ever be needed in the entire world. Today, modern information technology is on the verge of becoming a 'disposable product'; it is a consumable and encountered in almost every aspect of modern life.

The claim that computers are a new technology no longer holds true. Indeed, computers are actually a mature and stable form of technology. The 'rapid advances' which are often referred to in fact tend to reflect increased operating speed and storage capacity, provided at a stable or decreasing cost.

Sometimes new technology is introduced, such as color liquid crystal displays for portable computers, but in the vast majority of cases the advances do not provide additional functionality.

It is true that the technology is a moving target, but the nature of the tasks performed has remained largely unchanged over a surprisingly long period. Many computing tools are fundamentally unchanged in function, merely presented in a different wrapping.

For example, word-processing as an activity has moved from being a centralised remote activity (on a minicomputer) to a decentralised local activity (on a desk-top PC), and is now showing signs of moving to an intermediate configuration of combined centralised and distributed activity with word-processors provided on networked file servers.

These variations refer only to the *implementation* of the activities. The tasks themselves are largely unchanged: users still want features such as paragraph handling, page numbering, block and character manipulation, and spell-checking.

Therefore, the way in which technology is used for data processing tasks has not changed significantly. Instead, wide-spread usage of computer facilities has been relocated onto the desk-top, and then enhanced. Accordingly, organizations should be able to draw upon much greater and more widely-available levels of expertise. This would be applied to the introduction of computer technology for more rapid data processing and more comprehensive information availability.

Thus it is now time to admit that computer specialists of all kinds - analysts, designers and scientists - should have a better understanding and awareness of the problems and issues, if not an initial grasp on possible solutions.

It may still be suggested that it is impossible to predict where technology advances may take us. Nevertheless, all that has really happened within the last ten years is that data processing can now be achieved in a localised environment and at a vastly greater rate than before. This is why we can now make use of Graphic User Interfaces or multimedia systems.

The urgency to correct this misperception becomes all the greater when we realise the risks and dangers of *not* thinking about where we are being taken by our runaway technology. We should take heed of the fact that today's 'power-users' are actually in control of super-charged technology, and drive their efforts using 'pedal-power' principles. It is not surprising that there should be an ever-increasing need for computer security controls.

The effectiveness of controls

In most cases, implementation of security measures is a matter of identifying appropriate controls and ensuring that they are applied fully within the defined protection domains.

While a number of practical controls exist that may be implemented to facilitate any form of security, it is inevitable that some controls must be developed which are more specific to information systems. Such controls include:

- Development controls, which relate to the environment within which the information system is designed, constructed, tested and maintained.
- Operational system controls, which are limits imposed by the system regardless of user or application.
- Internal controls, which are application user-specific controls, such as access limitations for database tasks.

A number of mechanisms exist for implementing information system controls, including hardware components, encryption, and limitations on information dissemination. The major characteristic of such controls is that they will directly affect each and every user, and as such will often be the means by which the set of security measures are judged. Ease of use for the information system and effectiveness of security measures are therefore competing requirements.

While controls are mechanisms which are built into the system, and hence cannot normally be bypassed by users, policies are mechanisms which are not built in, and hence have an element of voluntary compliance by all users. Good examples are regular backups of data, and changing passwords regularly. Neither of these require any additional information system mechanisms, but can dramatically improve the overall integrity of the system. Clearly, legal and ethical policies are important examples, but are unlikely to be as dependable as other means.

Controls and policies are of no value unless they are applied and used properly. Three clearly identifiable factors will contribute to the application and proper use of such controls or policies.

The first is the awareness and appreciation of the problems. People functioning within the constraints of the controls or policies must be aware of the need for them, and further, they must be convinced of their value. This will only happen if it is understood why a particular measure is appropriate for the specific situation.

Unfortunately, many users will be unaware of the security needs of an information system, particularly if the tasks being performed were previously the domain of another department or facility.

A good example can be observed in the poor application of security and backup measures within the PC environment. By contrast, larger systems are more likely to have full and adequate backup facilities that are the responsibility of operational staff.

The second factor is the likelihood of use. An otherwise satisfactory mechanism is of little value if it is not used. Fire doors which are wedged open to facilitate easy passage are a good example of this.

In order to help deal with problems of misapplication, or bypassing the controls altogether, it is sensible to consider overlapping controls, or redundancy in the mechanisms. This also builds upon the strengths of having alternative mechanisms for the same situation, as well as allowing a mechanism to be applied in more than one circumstance.

The third and final factor is that to be successful, controls and policies will require the full support of staff in the organization. They must implement the checks and controls, not merely by following the letter, but by supporting the concept of those checks.

The use of standard solutions

In the light of this, we may even be approaching the point at which it is meaningful to begin to identify 'standard' solutions to problems. As more examples of computer security problems are identified by specialists, so it becomes a realistic process to identify appropriate calculations whereby the time required for complete recovery can be identified, according to the size and nature of the data reconstruction. Representatives within the organization can then simply choose between several possible options (which differ primarily in reconstruction time) according to how urgent it is that the system be available again.

However, it is not actually necessary to carry out risk assessment in order to implement security measures. Experienced security specialists will already know sensible measures and precautions to take. An expensive assessment of all possible risks and threats would be unlikely to contribute anything new, and the time and resources could be much better spent on implementing the practical solutions.

The major example of computer security violation concerns the generic problem of theft of information. Just as any home should be protected by sensible measures such as door locks, bolts and alarms; so computer-based information systems can be protected by prudent application of existing techniques for data protection and domain partitioning. These techniques are continually evolving and improving as further research is carried out in operating systems and applications systems technology.

From computer security to systems integrity

When we consider the specific problem of what constitutes computer security, it is hard to avoid wondering whether the term itself is a misnomer. There is little point in providing excessive security for a computer system, because that is simply a hardware entity that - increasingly - is standardized, and can often be insured as a physical device.

The more difficult but urgent objective should be to provide protection for the material that the computer processes and stores on behalf of the owner organization: data. At the very least, therefore, we should be talking about data security rather than computer security.

Next, we observe that the threats to information systems will be greatest when perpetrated by people who gain access to the system. It is true that computers can quickly delete or modify very large quantities of data. However, in most cases judicious application of backup and documentation techniques will prove more than sufficient to protect against such forms of accidental damage. Nevertheless, there are few mechanisms or procedures that can provide satisfactory and cost-effective protection against deliberate, malicious or premeditated actions by users.

This leads us to suggest that the concept of integrity, as normally applied under the CIA model, is not complete. We can conceive of situations where the integrity of the technology remains viable, but non-technological integrity fails. This introduces weaknesses into the system.

Going further, it may even be the case that the CIA model leads us to address only a subset of the issues. Although the CIA concepts are clearly of very great importance to the idea of security, there are a number of other contributory factors.

These include such ideas as the locality of the protection or secure systems domain, the privileges which are accorded to users or which may be applied to information systems objects, the relevance of the objects and their protection levels, and above all the overall assurance that the security of the system is both as specified and as described.

Locality refers to a better understanding of the partitioning of domains within the information system, and forms a counterpart to the concept of relevance within the system. Clearly, there are situations and objects for which it is impossible to determine the actual degree of protection that is required. An obvious solution is to assume the highest agreed level as a safe default. In practical terms, we are beginning to identify groups or levels of protection, and this may be addressed under the concept of locality.

The need for privacy and privilege control is distinct from confidentiality, which perhaps implies the existence of mechanisms to assess and then provide for the sharing of information.   By contrast, privacy has a perspective of preventing the sharing of information.

Regardless of any protection mechanisms installed in most computer-based information systems, the system manager or administrator is, effectively, omnipotent. It is extremely difficult to establish a mechanism whereby such a 'super-user' status can both be firmly restricted, and yet remains guaranteed to be secure in itself.

A further major problem is that, owing to the inherent danger of un-reliability in many computer systems, there is often a requirement for a method of gaining super-user access via equivalent privileges on other machines.

In other words, it may be desirable and even necessary to provide privilege mechanisms by which powerful levels of access and control may be obtained, and yet provision of such facilities is a means to undermine the security that is desired.

The relevance of the material or objects to be protected or secured is important in order to determine the amount of material that must be protected, and to what degree.

For example, a directory containing computer games - and which should not be on the system anyway - should not be eligible for protection mechanisms. And yet, *not* providing security mechanisms may make this a loophole through which system penetration may be achieved.

Security mechanisms may be applied by naive users - which can include novice system administrators - on an indiscriminate basis.   This has two implications.

Firstly, the security mechanisms, which perhaps require expensive resources, are being wasted on items that do not need securing.

Secondly, if minimal thought is given to the relevance of protection for objects, then the protection mechanisms will become devalued in the eyes of those who must apply them and work within them.

Also of relevance is the nature of the controls, and any potential conflict with social or functional aspects. The controls themselves must be carefully considered, as must the selection of those who will identify, implement and enforce them.

A draconian set of controls may well be highly effective in protecting objects and systems, but some of this protection may also result from the fact that otherwise authorized users are unable to use the system appropriately or effectively.

The possible weaknesses arising from the simplicity of the CIA model indicates that we need a more consistent and comprehensive understanding of security. As has been suggested, it may even be appropriate to question the use of the term 'computer security'. Using technology to disseminate information beyond its normally permissible boundaries is clearly a breakdown of security.

But at what point does the technology become computer technology? Documented cases illustrate that a fax machine may be used to 'leak' information. Presumably most people would dispute the assertion that a fax machine is a computer. Yet with the advent of so-called 'fax-cards', which are hardware extensions to computers that may even be available as a shared resource across networks, the distinction becomes much less clear-cut.

Such a trivial example becomes more important when we try to allocate responsibility to domains. For example, would all fax machines - however implemented, installed or located - fall into the domain of responsibility for computer personnel or more generalised staff? There might be advantages and disadvantages to either. Indeed, the implications of such distinctions may well be significant for legislative and insurance purposes.

Our conclusion is that there is an urgent need to reconsider the problem of perception. The value of this would be in encouraging alternative, and hopefully more productive, perceptions of the issues of security of information systems. Not least, this means that we must consider people and information technology interaction as part of the problem. Such an approach requires and recommends addressing the problem from a wider perspective, and in particular one that is better suited to the environment under consideration.

This is a role where managers have an essential part to play. As well as their understanding of the staff, they are in a better position to have a greater overall view of the issues, as highlighted in chapter four. Their perception of security problems will necessarily reflect and influence the way in which the greatest weaknesses and strengths of computer systems are identified.

Indeed, it may even be appropriate to redefine the terms of the problems away from emphasis upon computer security, and instead to recognise the problem as being one that relates to a concept of *systems integrity*.

For the first part of the redefinition, which is where we move from 'computer' to 'system', we can observe that some of the essential concepts in dealing with computer security problems do not actually involve computers at all.

For example, educating users and indeed all employees to question strangers who are seen searching through discarded piles of computer printout is not a technological problem. Extending the domain beyond computers up to all systems that include and comprise computers, we are able to consider the problems in their environments.

In one particular case, environmental factors appeared to play a considerable role in the problems being experienced. A large computer user on the south coast of Britain encountered considerable problems with computer systems crashing and failing unexpectedly.

In an attempt to identify the problem, power supply monitors were installed, computer hardware was replaced, and all staff activities were logged. Much of the computer equipment was returned to the manufacturers for thorough testing, but no faults could be found. It was only when special shielding equipment was installed in the computer rooms that the problems began to diminish.

It was subsequently claimed that the source of the problems was from the powerful radar transmission systems on ships situated at a nearby Navy base. The radar systems were thought to be emitting sufficiently powerful waves of electromagnetic energy to interfere with some of the delicate electronics of otherwise reliable technology.

An even simpler example was identified by a large bank which thought it had found the ideal location for a major data processing centre, at the nexus of a major communications junction, enabling quick and easy access to the capital. However, when the extensive sets of disk drives were installed, continual failures and errors were eventually traced to vibration in the building due to the ever-increasing traffic nearby.

Turning now to the second part of the redefinition, from 'security' to 'integrity', the use or emphasis on 'securing' seems to have a distinctly defensive connotation, whereas a more constructive approach may be to adopt an actively preventative or 'offensive' posture.

The implication of security is that there is an external threat of some kind, against which an entity must be protected. Thinking of security subconsciously introduces the idea of protective measures such as (in physical terms) fences, or alarms.

Use of the term security may subconsciously influence decisions regarding other considerations, in particular by suggesting a defensive approach to some problems. Yet an active approach may be more suitable.

For example, in an ideal world it would be possible to provide a variety of mechanisms for systems protection with sufficient redundancy and overlap to make the need to backup data regularly a superfluous process. In other words an active preventative approach to the problem would be taken to ensure that the need to restore information from backups never arises.

At present, a security-aware organization has little choice but to implement an efficient and effective backup and recovery mechanism for its computer systems. However, no matter how quick and easy to use the backup service may be, each instance of its use must represent use of time and resources that could be allocated for more productive activities.

This is yet another reason for discarding the term 'security' with its implication in this context of computer dependence. It is possible that one day the term 'computer security' may be abandoned in favour of an alternative such as 'systems integrity'.

Consideration of the many examples of computer security problems soon reveals that, for the majority of cases, it is the non-technology components of information systems that provide the primary sources of major computer-related security breakdowns. Computer systems are truly binary devices: they either work or they do not. But the environment of the system can introduce an enormous number of influencing factors which can result in an infinite variety of combinations of effects and circumstances. These cannot be evaluated or quantified so easily.

For example, computer operators are always in a position to 'modify' tasks for their own benefit. That benefit may be to exact revenge upon more senior colleagues, or to introduce a problem and then appear to solve it, thus earning praise and hopefully reward. At a lower level within the system, software developers can include secret access mechanisms, using software or even hardware, so that at a later date they can gain unrestricted access quickly and easily.

Most computer programmers are capable of inserting destructive commands to achieve some form of employment protection. Functional or non-computing staff could compose valid directives or instructions for processing data, but which include additional commands, or modify existing procedures, for personal gain.

As a final observation, we may tentatively suggest that the technical implementation of security of computer-based information systems is not actually a difficult topic in itself. The problems that must be overcome in implementing various encryption, backup and audit trail systems are increasingly clear-cut and well understood; and the solutions are correspondingly varied and comprehensive.

The real difficulty in addressing computer security arises with regard to the scope of the problems that are considered, and the environment within which the problems are defined and must be faced. This underlines the need for a wider perspective on the problem domain, which incorporates not just the techno-specific considerations, but the effects of implementation of proposed solutions, the effects upon the organizational functions, and the effects upon all organizational staff.

Summary

An interesting characteristic of businesses and management theorists is the predilection for fashionable concepts. In the past, these have included total quality management, time-based competition, and change management. One idea that appears to be gaining ground at the current time is the concept of the Learning Organization.

This builds upon the observation that in an age when quality, technology and variety are becoming widely available to all organizations at comparatively low cost, the only remaining area where competitive advantage can be gained and maintained is in the ability to learn faster than its rivals, and be more successful at predicting changes in the business environment.

In order to achieve this, the learning organization must encourage continuous development of knowledge at all levels. Importantly, this means that organizations must implement mechanisms for moving that knowledge around quickly and easily, to where it is required. From there, the knowledge can be applied to change the way that the organization functions and reacts, both internally and externally.

The underlying framework of the learning organization is the need for generating, distributing and applying knowledge. This suggests a need for information systems, and in particular information systems which are computer-based.

The author makes no judgement on the concept of the learning organization, other than to observe that it is yet another indication of the growing importance of information systems to organizations. In particular, the accuracy, performance and relevance of the systems must be seen as crucial. Accordingly, the importance of the systems must be more widely appreciated, as must the need to protect and secure those systems.

Protection mechanisms are frequently technology-based. But as information systems pervade the organization, so the protection of those systems becomes more complex, depending less upon technology and more upon systemic perception. Earlier in this book, we described the problem of the technology trap. Even when forewarned, organizations may find it very difficult to construct a winning scenario to avoid the trap. It is not easy to break even, although it may be possible. But as with most other aspects of business, there is no choice - you have to play. The secret of success is to appreciate that the best moves are not built upon technology alone, but require application of management skills.

Bibliography

The Art of War. Sun Tzu (translation by Samuel B. Griffith). Oxford University Press, 1963. ISBN 0-19-501476-6

Building a Secure Computer System. Morrie Gasser. Van Nostrand Reinhold, 1988. ISBN 0-442-230222-2

Business Information: Systems and Strategies. Carol Cashmore and Richard Lyall. Prentice-Hall International, 1991. ISBN 0-13-552712-0

Commonsense Computer Security. Martin R. Smith. McGraw-Hill, 1989. ISBN 0-07-707162-X

Computer Ethics. T. Forester and P. Morrison. Blackwell, 1990. ISBN 0-631-17242-4

Computer Networks. Andrew S. Tanenbaum. Prentice-Hall International, 1989. ISBN 0-13-166836-6

Computer-related Crime: Analysis of Legal Policy. Organization for Economic Co-operation and Development, 1986. ISBN 92-64-12852-2

Computers Under Attack: Intruders, Worms, and Viruses. Ed: Peter J. Denning. Addison-Wesley Publishing Company, 1990. ISBN 0-201-53067-8

Criminal Law: Computer Misuse. The Law Commission. Her Majesty's Stationery Office, 1989. ISBN 0-10-108192-8

The Cuckoo's Egg. Clifford Stoll. Pan Books, 1991. ISBN 0-330-31742-3

Cyberpunk: Outlaws and Hackers on the Computer Frontier. K. Hafner and J. Markoff. Fourth Estate, 1991. ISBN 1-872180-94-9

Datapro Reports on Information Security International. Datapro Information Services Group. McGraw-Hill, 1992

The Data Protection Act 1984: Guideline 2: The Definitions, Second series. The Office of the Data Protection Registrar, February 1989.

Data Theft: Computer fraud, industrial espionage and information crime. Hugo Cornwall. Heinemann, London, 1987. ISBN 0-434-90265-9

Designing Information Systems Security. R. Baskerville. Wiley, 1988. ISBN 0-471-91772-9

Fraudbusting. David Price. Mercury Books, 1991. ISBN 1-85251-089-7

The Industrial Espionage Handbook. Hugo Cornwall. Random Century Ltd, 1991. ISBN 0-7126-3634-X

Industrial Espionage: Intelligence Techniques and Countermeasures. Norman R. Bottom, Jr. and Robert R. J. Gallati. Butterworth Publishers 1984. ISBN 0-409-95108-0

Information Technology and the Law, Second Edition. Editors: Chris Edwards, Nigel Savage and Ian Walden. Macmillan Publishers Ltd, 1990. ISBN 0-333-53150-7

Information Technology Security Evaluation Criteria (ITSEC). Luxembourg: Office for Official Publications of the European Communities, 1991. ISBN 92-826-3004-8. Catalogue number: CD-71-91-502-EN-C

Hacker's Handbook III. Hugo Cornwall. Century Hutchinson Ltd, 1988. ISBN 0-7126-1147-9

Information Anxiety. Richard Saul Wurman. Pan Books, 1991. ISBN 0-330-31097-6

Information Systems for Business. D. S. Hussain and K. M. Hussain. Prentice Hall, 1991. ISBN 0-13-463647-3

Management, Second Edition. James A. F. Stoner and R. Edward Freeman. Prentice-Hall International, 1989. ISBN 0-13-551672-2

Management Information Systems. David Kroenke. McGraw-Hill International, 1989. ISBN 0-07-100515-3

Managing Data Protection. C. Pounder, M. Kosten, S. Papadopoulos and A. Rickard. The Chartered Institute of Public Finance and Accountancy, 1987. ISBN 0-85299-366-8

Organizational Computer Security Policies. Adrian R. Warman. Department of Information Systems, London School of Economics. July 1991

Password Security: A Case History. Robert Morris and Ken Thompson. Communications of the ACM, Vol. 22, No. 11., November 1979

Security of Computer Based Information Systems. V. P. Lane. Macmillan, 1985. ISBN 0-333-36437-6

Security for Computer Networks, Second Edition. D. W. Davies and W. L. Price. Wiley, 1989. ISBN 0-471-92137-8

Security in Computing. Charles P. Pfleeger. Prentice-Hall International, 1989. ISBN 0-13-799016-2

Systems Management. Andrew Parkin. Arnold, 1987. ISBN 0-7131-2815-1

Trusted Computer System Evaluation Criteria. US Department of Defense. DOD 5200.28-STD

X/Open Security Guide. X/Open Company, Ltd. Prentice-Hall, 1989. ISBN 0-13-972142-8

Index